Perspectives on Strategy

Perspectives on Strategy
Contributions of
Michael E. Porter

Edited by

F.A.J. VAN DEN BOSCH
Erasmus Universiteit Rotterdam

and

A.P. DE MAN
Erasmus Universiteit Rotterdam

KLUWER ACADEMIC PUBLISHERS
BOSTON / DORDRECHT / LONDON

A C.I.P. Catalogue record for this book is available from the Library of Congress.

ISBN 0-7923-9895-5 (HB)
ISBN 0-7923-9896-3 (PB)

Published by Kluwer Academic Publishers,
P.O. Box 17, 3300 AA Dordrecht, The Netherlands.

Kluwer Academic Publishers incorporates
the publishing programmes of
D. Reidel, Martinus Nijhoff, Dr W. Junk and MTP Press.

Sold and distributed in the U.S.A. and Canada
by Kluwer Academic Publishers,
101 Philip Drive, Norwell, MA 02061, U.S.A.

In all other countries, sold and distributed
by Kluwer Academic Publishers,
P.O. Box 322, 3300 AH Dordrecht, The Netherlands.

Printed on acid-free paper

Contents

1.

Introduction: Perspectives on Porter

F.A.J. van den Bosch

Relevance of Strategy research: focus on Michael Porter's contributions
Strategy is a fascinating field of enquiry, both for managers looking for
a sustainable competitive advantage and for academic researchers
looking for the reasons behind superior firm performance. Strategy can
be a fascinating field of mutual learning as well, if practitioners and
researchers communicate with each other, exchange ideas and findings
and try to understand each other's perspective. Such a cross-
fertilization can improve the relevance of strategy theory and of the
managerial instruments grounded in it. From time to time we, as
strategy researchers, need to assess the relevance of our research by
stepping back and asking ourselves if we are on track and whether
practitioners still share our findings. Or as Hamel and Prahalad (1996:
242) recently asked: "So, just how relevant is the corpus of knowledge
we call 'strategic management' to the new information economy?".

In principle such an assessment can be done in a number of ways. For
example, by analyzing key contributions to the strategy field from a
managerial perspective, by confronting CEO's from multinational
enterprises with academic research and asking them to reflect on its
relevance, or by asking top managers whether they are depending on

1

F.A.J. van den Bosch and A.P. de Man (eds.), Perspectives on Strategy, 1-6.
© 1997 *Kluwer Academic Publishers. Printed in the Netherlands.*

academic research to answer their key questions. Another possibility is to assess the relevance of strategy research by focusing on the contribution over time by one of the leading scholars in the strategy field.

This last approach is what has been undertaken here in looking at the work carried out by Michael Porter, one of the most cited authors in strategy-oriented, leading academic journals in the field and, one of the most well known academic gurus. In this book academic evaluations of Porter's work are jointly presented with the views of Dutch practitioners on his oeuvre.

Strategy: content, context and process

Although Porter's work does not represent the whole strategy field, it is related to major parts of it. To illustrate this point, it is worthwhile distinguishing *three dimensions* of strategy. First, the strategy context dimension, which deals with the question of how the internal and external context (i.e. the industry, region, nation, etc.) of firms influences strategy. Second, the strategy content dimension, or the "what" of strategy, which refers to strategy as a specific "product" such as an acquisition to enhance existing competencies. Third, the strategy process dimension, or the "how" of strategy, which deals with the organizational processes used in arriving at a certain strategy.

Table 1.1:   *Three dimensions of strategy: strategy context, strategy content and strategy process and some contributions by Porter*

Context	Content	Process
The context of strategy	*The what of strategy*	*The how of strategy*
Five Forces Framework (Porter, 1980) Diamond Framework (Porter, 1990)	Value Chain Framework (Porter, 1985) Corporate Strategy Framework (Porter, 1987)	

Source: Author; for the distinction between strategy context, strategy content and strategy process see De Wit & Meyer (1994).

Table 1.1 illustrates that Porter in particular contributes to the first two dimensions of strategy: context and content. For example, the widely used Five Forces Framework (see chapters 2 and 3) is a typical example of a framework describing the context dimension of strategy; in this case the influence of the industry environment on the competitive strategy of the firm. Although the firm can use this framework as an input for strategy formation and in particular for formulating the strategy content, the framework, as such, is more related to context than to content. Table 1.1 reveals a remarkable fact: Porter's contributions, as is the case for the majority of the contributions of other leading scholars in the field, are primarily concentrated within the context and content dimensions and not in the process dimension. I will come back to this observation later on in chapter 10 in which Porter's contribution to a dynamic theory of strategy will be sketched.

Purpose of this book
The *purpose of this book* is to focus on the contribution of one of the most prominent scholars in the strategy field, Michael Porter, from both a practitioner, that is Chief Executive Officer (CEO), perspective, and from a research perspective. Using such a *dual perspective* may improve the relevance of strategy research for the business community.

The immediate cause for this book was the awarding of an Honorary Degree to Michael Porter by the Erasmus University Rotterdam, at the proposal of the Faculty of Business Administration/Rotterdam School of Management, November 1993. To celebrate this important event a symposium entitled "Creating Competitive Advantage: strategies at the business, corporate, regional and national level" was organized by the department of Strategy and Business Environment of the Rotterdam School of Management.

Four leading chief executives, two from European multinationals (Royal Dutch/Shell Group and Unilever N.V.) and two from important Dutch public organizations (the Port of Rotterdam and the Ministry of Economic Affairs), were invited to reflect on Porter's contributions to four levels of analysis. Respectively these levels are: (1) business level strategy, (2) corporate level strategy, (3) regional competitiveness and finally (4) national competitiveness. These four levels of analysis represent different though overlapping levels of strategy and address one or more of the dimensions of strategy. The first two levels are company or inside-out oriented, the last two are outside-in oriented that is more related to the context dimension of strategy, or to the business environment. Both orientations are related to the core activity of strategy: aligning a company with its changing business environment, or as Michael Porter defined this in the opening sentence of his first book on Competitive Strategy: "The essence of formulating competitive strategy is relating a company to its environment."

Stimulated by a successful symposium, the idea emerged to compose a book containing not only the reflections of the business community and public authorities on Porter's contribution but those of the strategy researchers as well. To this end, for each of the contributions of the practitioners, an accompanying introductory chapter by members of the Department of Strategic Management and Business Environment has been written. These introductory chapters have been written from a strategy research perspective and give a brief overview of Porter's contributions to that particular level of strategy as well as discussing a number of issues deserving further attention.

Content of this book

Against this background, the book is structured as follows (see table 1.2). Chapters 2 to 8 deal with the four mentioned levels of analysis from a dual perspective: theoretical and managerial. For example, Porter's key contributions to business level strategy are briefly described from a research perspective in chapter 2, and from a practitioner perspective in chapter 3. Due to the fact that Porter's diamond framework is applicable at both regional and national level, these levels are combined in one introductory chapter (chapter 6).

Table 1.2:   The structure of the book

Four levels of analysis in strategy research	From a research perspective	From a practitioner perspective
Business level	chapter 2	chapter 3
Corporate level	chapter 4	chapter 5
Regional level	chapter 6	chapter 7
National level	chapter 6	chapter 8

In the chapters 2-8, Porter's frameworks have been discussed at various levels of analysis. The two final chapters aim to find out how Porter's theories are related to each other and if and how the different levels of analysis can be connected (table 1.3 presents the core questions of the final chapters). Firstly, the question of how Porter's contributions are related to each other *over time* can be considered. Can we observe changes in his thinking or are his contributions closely related? Chapter 9 deals with some of the aspects of the relationships between Porter's contributions to strategy theory, focusing on three of his main publications. Secondly, observing the traditional distinction between the levels of analysis used in this book, an important question can be raised regarding the possibility of *connecting these levels of analysis* into one integrative framework. Is there a relation between these levels or should they be seen as separate? Chapter 10 deals with this second question by focusing on Porter's contributions to the development of a dynamic theory of strategy published in 1991.

Table 1.3:   Two core questions on Porter's contributions

1. How are Porter's contributions to strategy theory related to each other over time? (chapter 9)
2. How can the different levels of analysis studied by Porter be connected in one framework? (chapter 10)

Combined effort

As indicated above, the purpose of this book is to focus on the contribution of one of the most prominent scholars, Michael Porter, to the strategy field, and to examine this from both a practitioner perspective and a research perspective. I presume that using such a dual perspective can indeed improve the understanding of each perspective and therewith increase the relevance of strategy research for business. Whether this is the case, has to be judged by the readers. But I believe that making strategy research really work requires a combined effort and presents a mutual challenge for both strategy researchers and practitioners.

References

De Wit, B., R.J.H. Meyer (eds.), 1994, *Strategy Process, Content, Context: An International Perspective*, West, St. Paul.

Hamel, G., C.K. Prahalad, 1996, "Competing in the new economy: managing out of bounds", *Strategic Management Journal*, Vol. 17, 237-242.

Porter, M.E., 1980, *Competitive Strategy: Techniques for analyzing Industries and Competitors*, Free Press, New York.

Porter, M.E., 1985, *Competitive Advantage:Creating and Sustaining Superior Performance*, Free Press, New York.

Porter, M.E., 1987, "From Competitive Advantage to Corporate Strategy", *Harvard Business Review*, May-June, p. 43-59.

Porter, M.E., 1990, *The Competitive Advantage of Nations*, MacMillan, London.

Porter, M.E., 1991, "Towards a dynamic theory of strategy", *Strategic Management Journal*, Vol. 12, pp. 95-117.

2.

Porter on business strategy

Bob de Wit

Introduction

Although one author can hardly make a school, Porter's first book *Competitive Strategy* has had so much impact that it has stimulated a generation of researchers. For more than a decade Porter's positioning school (a name popularised by Mintzberg, 1990) has been the dominating school of thought in the strategy field. The name positioning school stems from Porter's central idea that a business should try to achieve 'competitiveness through positioning'. Positioning determines whether a firm's profitability is above or below the industry average. The basic assumption of Porter's positioning school is that the industry environment largely determines the firm's freedom to manoeuvre. The environment has far more influence on shaping firms' strategies than the other way around; a company should place most emphasis on adapting a company to its environment. Since the underlying logic of the positioning approach is to first understand the environment and next position the firm, it is also referred to as the *outside-in approach*.

Porter's outside-in approach is not surprising, since many of his ideas are based on the economics field of industrial organisation. Teece,

F.A.J. van den Bosch and A.P. de Man (eds.), Perspectives on Strategy, 7-18.

Pisano, and Shuen (1990) state: "This approach stems in part from the structure-conduct-performance paradigm of industrial organisation developed by Mason (1949), Bain (1959) and others, though it is considerably richer than that tradition." In particular, the structure-conduct-performance paradigm put more emphasis on structure (meaning context) than on conduct (meaning strategy), and more on the implications for public policy than for strategies of companies (Mintzberg, 1990). Porter's works demonstrate his fascination with competition, a fascination he shares with managers. His instant popularity is partly explained by his quest for models to help companies analyse and beat the competition. To use his own ideas, Porter proved to be successful in positioning himself in an emerging market. Or did he create his own environment?

Porter's writings on business strategy
Porter argues that competition occurs at the business unit level. It is therefore not surprising that most of his writings deal with the basis of strategy at the business level. Porter has published extensively on business level strategies. He has written an impressive number of articles, although his books *Competitive Strategy* and *Competitive Advantage* are best known. His second book, *Competitive Advantage, Creating and Sustaining Superior Performance* (1985) is an important contribution to our understanding of business strategy, although not a smash hit as *Competitive Strategy*. Both books have in common a number of powerful frameworks, highly useful tools that can be applied in many different situations. Both books make accessible a number of ideas originating in the economics literature. An important difference is that his first has primarily an external orientation, while the second book has predominantly an internal focus. The aim of the second book is to build a bridge between strategy and implementation. In this section the most important concepts from these two books will be discussed at length.

Porter's book *Competitive Strategy, Techniques for Analysing Industries and Competitors* (1980) provides a number of general analytical techniques, of which the structural analysis of industries, generic competitive strategies, and generic industry environments are best known and widely used. Appendix B of the book, that describes how to conduct an industry analysis, also appeared to be very useful. The main techniques are:

Five competitive forces model: For a structural analysis of industries Porter introduces his five-forces model. Five competitive forces acting upon an industry are described and analysed: bargaining power of suppliers and buyers, the threat of new entrants and substitute products, and rivalry among existing firms. He assumes a direct relationship between the strength of competitive forces and industry profitability. Companies that are successful in defending themselves against the competitive forces can anticipate above-average profits.

Generic competitive strategies: The five-forces framework is then used to identify the three generic competitive strategies to achieve a defendable competitive position. Porter argues that these generic strategies provide companies with the ability to achieve a competitive advantage and outperform other companies in their industry. The first generic strategy is the *cost leadership* strategy. Companies that produce at the lowest cost in the industry can charge the lowest prices, and get higher market share, or charge the same prices to receive higher profits than the competition. The second generic strategy, *differentiation*, strives for uniqueness in the industry as perceived by the buyers. Although differentiation involves higher costs (Porter, 1985), this strategy allows the company to charge higher prices. Finally, the *focus* strategy targets a particular market segment or a geographic segment where it is able to serve clients better than full-line producers. Porter distinguishes between cost focus and differentiation focus, since focused companies employ both options. Companies that fail to develop one of the three generic strategies, or attempt to combine them, are stuck-in-the-middle, and should anticipate below average profitability.

Generic industry environments: Porter introduced five generic industry environments. These environments differ on a number of key dimensions: industry concentration, state of industry maturity, and exposure to international competition. Porter describes five generic industry environments. Fragmented industries have a low level of industry concentration. Emerging, mature, and declining industries differ fundamentally on the state of maturity. Finally, global industries face international competition. In these generic industry environments, the crucial aspects of industry structure, key strategic issues, characteristic strategic alternatives, and strategic pitfalls are described.

How to conduct an industry analysis: Appendix B of the book describes how to conduct an industry analysis, and is especially useful for applying many of the ideas in the book. It provides an organized approach to actually conducting an industry study, including sources of field and published data as well as guidance in field interviewing.

The cornerstone of Porter's second important book on business strategy, *Competitive Advantage, Creating and Sustaining Superior Performance* (1985), is the value chain.

The value chain describes a business as a collection of interdependent activities, which in turn, form part of a continuous system that stretches back to suppliers and forward to channels and customers. The concept helps a firm to clarify the kinds of values it offers to buyers and suppliers over the competition. The value chain is comprised of primary and support activities. Primary activities are inbound logistics, operations, outbound logistics, marketing and sales, and service. The support activities, that span across all five of the primary activities, are firm infrastructure, human resource management, technology development, and procurement. Using the value chain framework, Porter suggests advantage can be captured through intensive efforts at improvement or reorganization of these value activities. In other words, companies should better organise the linkages between different primary and secondary activities in their businesses. This improvement of coordination can also extend outside the individual business, into the *value system* of an industry.

Empirical research based on Porter's work
The concepts of generic strategies have been subject to empirical research (Dess and Davis, 1984; Miller and Dess, 1993; Miller and Friesen, 1986; McNamee and McHugh, 1989; White, 1986), that provides some support. Dess and Davis (1984) empirically demonstrated the existence of strategic groups that conformed to Porter's generic strategies. They also showed that those firms following a generic strategy outperformed those with no clear-cut strategic orientation. Kim and Lim (1988) emphasized the empirical evidence that exists for Porter's strategy typology, arguing that the typology has received more support than other strategy constructs. Miller (1988) measured cost leadership by using items concerning cost control, price cutting, minimization of marketing and product development costs, and conservatism in responding to markets. He measured

differentiation through scales that assessed product innovation, new product development expenditures, strategic aggressiveness, and extensiveness of advertising. Focus was evaluated using variables such as number of product lines produced and degree of similarity between lines. He also pointed out (1991) that Porter's typology has been widely replicated (see also Huo and McKinley, 1992).

From this short overview it can be concluded that Porter has stimulated empirical research. Porter's relative impact on the strategy field can be derived from a quick review by Miller and Dess (1993). It learns that Porter's first book was referenced in approximately half of all of the articles in the *Strategic Management Journal* between 1986 and 1990.

An evaluation of Porter's contributions to business strategies
It seems fair to use Porter's own objectives while evaluating Porter's contributions to business strategy. In the introduction to his first book, *Competitive Strategy, Techniques for Analysing Industries and Competitors* (1980), Porter (1980: xv-xvi) considers his primary target group to be practitioners: "This book is written for practitioners, that is, managers seeking to improve the performance of their businesses..... The book is not written from the viewpoint of the scholar or in the style of my more academically oriented work, but it is hoped that scholars will nevertheless be interested in the conceptual approach, the extensions to the theory of industrial organization, and the many case examples." Porter's wish has become reality: the importance of Porter's contributions to business managers is illustrated by Shell's CEO Herkströter's contribution in the next chapter of this book.

Porter's contribution to management science is not limited to stimulating empirical research, as was discussed in the previous paragraph. Some new management concepts are based on, or at least influenced by, his concepts. For example, activity-based costing is an approach to cost accounting, considering costs from the perspective of subprocesses in the company's value chain. The essence of quality management is to examine the company's activities and subprocesses and make them work better. The concept of time-based competition is in its very essence finding ways of integrating and coordinating a series of activities within the company. These three concepts incorporate elements of the value chain or are based on it.

It is widely agreed that Porter's most successful book is his first, *Competitive Strategy, Techniques for Analysing Industries and Competitors* (1980). It contains a number of models that proved to be major contributions to our understanding of business strategy. The book was an immediate success and influenced practitioners and researchers alike. The concepts from his second book *Competitive Advantage: Creating and Sustaining Superior Performance* (1985) have had a major impact as well. The value chain and the value system are important concepts of managers' vocabulary, and have influenced further conceptual thinking.

Review of critiques
Works of great importance get criticisms, some of them quite legitimate. In fact, many critiques are implicit compliments. Take the following quote from Hamel and Prahalad's article *Strategic Intent* (1989): "Armed with concepts like segmentation, the value chain, competitor benchmarking, strategic groups, and mobility barriers, many managers have become better and better at drawing industry maps. But while they have been busy map making, their competitors have been moving entire continents." In other words, Porter's works are so influential that (a) every Western company knows how to make his analyses, and (b) many companies think that these concepts can replace strategic thinking, which is of course not meant by Porter. Nevertheless, a number of criticisms have been brought forward, and can be put into five categories: critiques on strategic concepts; the separation between thinking and acting; a bias toward the economic over the political; a bias toward conventional, big, established business; and the outside-in perspective in relation to a number of highly successful companies with an inside-out perspective.

Critiques on strategy concepts. Critiques focus on two subjects, Porter's strategic positions and the idea of stuck in the middle. First, Porter's position that a company has to choose between generic strategies has been challenged by Chrisman et al. (1988), Hill (1988), Jones and Butler (1988) and Murray (1988). It is argued that a company can, or indeed should, combine cost leadership with differentiation. Miller (1992) characterizes Porter's generic strategies as specialized strategies, that can easily lead to single-mindedness and overspecialization. He advocates a mixed strategy: one that combines aspects of differentiation with cost-effectiveness. Baden-Fuller and Stopford (1992) put this point more strongly: "Generic strategies are a fallacy. The best firms are striving all the time to reconcile the opposites. .... Given the enormous rewards that accrue to those who can resolve the dilemma of the opposites, it is not surprising that there are no lasting or enduring generic strategies." This quote not only challenges the generic strategies concept, but also the idea of being *stuck in the middle*, the second subject of criticism. A number of theoretical contributions have criticised the idea of 'stuck in the middle' as well, e.g. Hill (1988), Karnani (1984), Murray (1988).

Separation of thinking and acting. Sigmund Freud assumed that patients who know the origin of their mental disease are almost restored to health. Likewise, Harvard strategists assume that competent top managers having the right information after using the right techniques, will formulate the right strategies that 'only' have to be implemented. Both in psychology and the world of business, reality appeared to be much more complex. Mintzberg argues in his critique on the Design School (1990): "The implication that thinking stops when the strategy is decided on...... discourages adaptation *of* the strategy (as opposed to *within* the strategy). The high failure rate of deliberate strategies has generally been attributed to problems of implementation. ....the blame more typically belongs not in implementation, not even back in formulation itself, but in the very fact of having separated the two, and so impeding the natural processes of learning in an organization." With other Harvard colleagues, Porter separates thinking from acting, formulation from implementation. Porter's works concentrate on analysing and on conceptual models. In other words, Porter's work deals with the *strategy content* dimension rather than the strategy process (De Wit & Meyer, 1994).

It can be assumed that Porter favours an analytical planning process. For example, in one of his few publications on the strategy process he writes (1987): "The questions that good planning seeks to answer .... will never lose their relevance." And also: "Every company, whether diversified or not, should have a strategic plan for each of its businesses." It is his opinion that strategy formation should be an analytical process, facilitating strategic thinking. The aim of good planning should be to analyse the future direction of competition, the needs of the customer, the likely behaviour of competitors, and how to gain a competitive advantage (Porter, 1987). These are the questions that Porter has been focusing on in most of his work. He tends to consider a "proper planning process" as the link between thinking and implementing (Porter, 1987), which is understandable given his explicit preference for analytical techniques. But strategic thinking requires more than analysis only. Ohmae (1982), for example, states that "... successful business strategies result not from rigorous analysis but from a particular state of mind." Ohmae further argues that strategy is a thought process that is basically creative and intuitive rather than rational. Strategists do not reject analysis. "Great strategies ... call for technical mastery in the working out but originate in insights that are beyond the reach of conscious analysis." Ohmae does not criticise Porter explicitly, but from the above it can be concluded that Ohmae thinks that analysis supports thinking, and that strategic thinking is predominantly synthetic.

To conclude, Porter's separation of thinking and acting is criticised for three different though related reasons. First, the right diagnosis does not automatically lead to restored health. The healing process, hardly discussed by Porter, is at least as important. Second, the failure of strategies often relates to the separation of formulation and implementation. And third, successful business strategies require synthesis as well, whereas Porter mainly stresses analysis.

Bias toward the economic over the political. In Porter's works, the profit potential of firms is related to market power. Companies that gain market power can expect above average profits. The bargaining power of buyers and suppliers must be diminished. Porter's usage of the power issue remains purely economic, although "the book can easily be taken as a primer for political action. If profit really does lie in market power, then there are clearly more than competitive economic ways to gain and sustain that power" (Mintzberg, 1990). A clear example of a company that has used its political power for organisational purposes is Société Générale de Belgique (Pringle & Hover, 1991). The company had been established in 1822, and its headquarters were located at 30 Rue Royale which formed one side of a square, the other sides of which were occupied by the Belgian parliament building and the royal palace. SGB was a significant economic and cultural force in Belgium, and used that power for the sake of its many subsidiaries. For example, foreign companies were blocked from entering Belgian markets. Mintzberg (1990) argues that Porter "is oriented to the economic and especially the quantifiable, as opposed to the social or political or even nonquantifiable economic."

Bias toward conventional, big, established business. One of the consequences of Porter's quantifiable economic orientation is his preference for companies and industries of which hard data are available. These are, by nature, conventional established businesses, where analysts have already gathered those data. New companies and upcoming industries can only be analysed once they are established. Hamel and Prahalad (1989) argue that "competitor analysis focuses on the existing resources of present competitors. The only companies seen as a threat are those with the resources to erode margins and market share in the next planning period. Resourcefulness, the pace at which new competitive advantages are being built, rarely enters in."

His bias toward *big* companies is also observed by Mintzberg (1990), who notices that "Porter discusses at some length strategies to consolidate fragmented industries, but nowhere does he balance this with discussion of strategies to fragment consolidated industries (which is, of course, a favorite behavior of small firms). Porter also discusses in one section industries that are 'stuck' in a fragmented situation, but nowhere does he discuss ones that are stuck in a consolidated situation." The critics may overshoot their mark, but overall Porter prefers big over small.

Outside-in versus inside-out. Porter's point of departure, the industry, is challenged quite convincingly by Rumelt (1991). His study pointed out that only 8.3 percent of the differences in profitability between one business unit and another can be related to their choice of industry. As much as 46.4 percent was explained by strategy choice, while 44.5 percent of profitability remained unexplained. For this reason, Baden-Fuller and Stopford (1992) argue that "the firm matters, not the industry. .... In general, profitable industries are more profitable because they are populated by more imaginative and more creative businesses." In fact, many firms are among the world's best companies because they create industries, instead of analysing them. Mintzberg's example illuminates this point (1990): "Kodak might study the market for instant camera's, but Polaroid created that market." Porter recognizes this (1991): "The most successful firms are notable in employing imagination to define a *new* position, or find *new* value in whatever starting position they have" (italics by Porter). Polaroid is an example of a company that creates industries by having developed unique capabilities. They compete on heterogeneous instead of homogeneous resources. They are examples of inside-out competitors (as opposed to outside-in competitors), also called resource-based competitors. The *resource-based view* of the firm, also called (dynamic) capabilities-based perspective, assumes that companies should develop capabilities and competences first (inside), and then bring new products to markets (outside). Porter considers the resource-based view as a promising stream of research (1991), although he argues that "the resource-based view cannot be an alternative theory of strategy. It cannot be separated from the cross-sectional determinants of competitive advantage or, for that matter, from the conception of the firm as a collection of activities. Stress on resources must complement, not substitute for, stress on market positions." Part of the inside-out versus outside-in debate is about *causality direction*. Porter recognizes this point. For example, he raises the questions (1991): "Should the environment be taken as given or not? Is the firm's scale an outcome or a cause?" These fundamental questions could be the start of a new stream of research.

Conclusion

The conclusion that must be drawn from this overview is that Porter's writings on business strategy are extensive and influential. He created a new school of thought in the strategy field, the positioning school, and introduced a number of presently well-known concepts such as the five forces model, generic strategies, and the value chain. Porter stimulated a generation of researchers. Empirical research in various countries has supported most of his ideas. Like most works of great importance, Porter's writings also got criticisms, such as his bias toward the economic over the political, and his bias toward conventional, big, established business. Porter not only stimulated the academic world, he also influenced a generation of managers. Practitioners, Porter's primary target group of his first book, have been very positive about Porter's contribution to our understanding of business strategy, as will be illustrated by Shell's CEO Herkströter in the next chapter.

References

Baden-Fuller, C. W. F., and J. Stopford (1992), *Rejuvenating the Mature Business*, London: Routledge.

Bain, J.S. (1959), *Industrial Organization*, New York: John Wiley.

Chrisman, J.J., C.W. Hofer, and W.R. Boulton (1988), "Toward a system for classifying business strategies", *Academy of Management Review*, No. 13, pp. 413-428.

Dess, G.G., and P.S. Davis (1984), "Porter's generic strategies as determinants of strategic group membership and organizational performance", *Academy of Management Journal*, No. 27, pp. 467-488.

De Wit, B. & R. Meyer (1994), *Strategy - Process, Content, Context: An International Perspective*, St. Paul: West Publishing.

Hamel, G. and C.K. Prahalad (1989), "Strategic Intent", *Harvard Business Review*, May-June, pp. 63-76.

Hill, C.W.L. (1988), "Differentiation versus low cost or differentiation and low cost: a contingency framework", *Academy of Management Review*, No. 13, pp. 401-412.

Huo, Y.P. & W. McKinley (1992), "Nation as a Context for Strategy: The Effects of National Characteristics on Business-Level Strategies", *Management International Review*, Vol. 32, No. 2, pp. 103-113.

Jones, G.R., and J.E. Butler (1988), "Costs, revenue, and business-level strategy", *Academy of Management Review*, No. 13, pp. 202-213.

Karnani, A. (1984), "Generic Competitive Strategies - An Analytical Approach", *Strategic Management Journal*, Vol. 5, pp. 367-380.

Kim, L., and Y. Lim (1988), "Environment, generic strategies, and performance in a rapidly developing country: a taxonomic approach", *Academy of Management Journal*, No. 31, pp. 802-827.

Mason, E. (1949), "The Current State of the Monopoly Problem in the U.S.", *Harvard Law Review*, June.

McNamee, P., and M. McHugh (1989), "Competitive Strategies in the Clothing Industry", *Long Range Planning*, Vol. 22, No. 4, pp. 63-71.

Miller, A. and G.G. Dess (1993), "Assessing Porter's (1980) model in terms of its generalizability, accuracy and simplicity", *Journal of Management Studies*, Vol. 30, No. 4, pp. 553-585.

Miller, D. (1988), "Relating Porter's business strategies to environment and structure: analysis and performance implications", *Academy of Management Journal*, No. 31, pp. 280-308.

Miller, D. (1991), "Stale in the saddle: CEO tenure and the match between organization and environment", *Management Science*, No. 37, pp. 34-52.

Miller, D. (1992), "The Generic Strategy Trap", *Journal of Business Strategy*, January/ February, pp. 37-41.

Miller, D., and P.H. Friesen (1986), "Porter's Generic Strategies and Performance: an Empirical Examination with American Data. Part 2: Performance Implications", *Organisation Studies*, Vol. 7, No. 3, pp. 255-261.

Mintzberg, H. (1990), "Strategy Formation: Schools of Thought", in J.W. Frederickson (ed), *Perspectives on Strategic Management*, New York: Harper & Row.

Murray, A.I. (1988), "A contingency view of Porter's generic strategies", *Academy of Management Review*, No 13, pp. 390-400.

Ohmae, K. (1982), *The Mind of the Strategist*, McGraw Hill.

Porter, M.E. (1980), *Competitive Strategy, Techniques for Analysing Industries and Competitors*, New York: Free Press.

Porter, M.E. (1985), *Competitive Advantage: Creating and Sustaining Superior Performance*, New York: Free Press.

Porter, M.E. (1987), "Corporate Strategy; the state of strategic thinking", *The Economist*, May.

Pringle, J.J., and D.H. Hover (1991), "Société Générale de Belgique", in De Wit, B. & R. Meyer (1994), *Strategy - Process, Content, Context: An International Perspective*, St. Paul: West Publishing.

Rumelt, R. (1991), "How Much Does Industry Matter?", *Strategic Management Journal*, March, pp. 167-186.

Teece, D.J., G. Pisano, and A. Shuen (1990), "Firm capabilities, resources, and the concept of strategy", *CCC Working Paper* No. 90-8, University of Berkeley.

White, R.E. (1986), "Generic Business Strategies, Organisational Context and Performance: an Empirical Investigation", *Strategic Management Journal*, Vol. 7, pp. 217-231.

3.

Business level strategy: Lessons from Shell

C.A.J. Herkströter (CEO, Royal Dutch/Shell)

Michael Porter is a leading academic, successful business consultant, an inspirational speaker, and a respected art collector. That Michael Porter did not become a professional golfer was that sport's loss - but for the Fortune 500 most fortunate indeed! Many of his ideas are of relevance to the business world. He is a profound thinker on matters about which Shell feels strongly. And it is particularly those of his ideas that have found practical application in the hard nosed world of business, that I wish to recall here.

Who can doubt that he has had an impact? The Economist, in August 1990, suggested that the market for management gurus is much like that for consumer brands: there is room for only a handful in the customer's mind. Among general thinkers about strategy only four can command world-wide attention - and earnings. Michael Porter is one of them. Tom Peters is another. And Peters paid Michael Porter a remarkable compliment when he sent a copy of *The Competitive Advantage of Nations* to every one of the 535 United States Congressmen, in order better to inform that country's legislators on what it takes to make a nation successful.

F.A.J. van den Bosch and A.P. de Man (eds.), Perspectives on Strategy, 19-24.
© 1997 *Kluwer Academic Publishers. Printed in the Netherlands.*

This book will be discussed in later chapters; I will confine myself to Porter's first book, *Competitive Strategy*, which was published in 1980. It made his name immediately. It has been translated into over a dozen languages and has passed its 35th printing. In this book, - and in his 1985 book, *Competitive Advantage*, - he pulled together a widely scattered literature on the nature of competition. He added his own research findings, and he presented a coherent and comprehensive approach to analyzing the market place. It is an approach which businessmen can actually use. It is Michael Porter's practical approach that managers at the business level have found so useful, even if some of them sometimes forget the obvious: "there is no point," said Porter, "in having a competitive strategy unless it produces competitive advantage!".

Generic strategies

Porter proposed three generic competitive strategies, three archetypal choices which businessmen face (see figure 3.1):

* to be the cost leader in his industry;
* to differentiate and thus offer premium value to customers; or
* to focus tightly on a market niche where competitors cannot erode profitability.

Figure 3.1: Generic Strategies

COMPETITIVE ADVANTAGE

		Lower Cost	**Differentiation**
COMPETITIVE SCOPE	**Broad Target**	Cost Leadership	Differentiation
	Narrow Target		Focus

Source: Porter (1980)

Many have said that this oversimplifies a complex situation, and Porter would agree that there are many variations on these themes. But by formulating his generic strategies in the way that he did, he provoked managers into thinking seriously about what the strategic choices were that they faced. It is at the business unit level, in the market place, that guilder by guilder, a corporation's profits are actually won. Porter's ideas made managers ask themselves what it was that customers valued and how that value could be created. Porter's theory enables them to argue sensibly about the implications of seeking cost leadership, and of differentiating their product offerings, and of attempting to identify and colonise market niches.

In this way Michael Porter created a new vocabulary for business. Indeed, one author has suggested that Porter is a little like Carolus Linnaeus, the Swedish botanist who developed a taxonomy of plants and animals. Porter's work, he himself thinks, might be of value as much for how he defines and describes the phenomenon of "competitiveness" as anything else. I suggest that it is this very utility, this practical usefulness, with which he presents his ideas - albeit somewhat copiously - that has made him the success at the business level that he has been and as we have found him, in practice, in the Royal Dutch/Shell Group of Companies.

Porter might even be called a Darwinian. He is always asking how a business relates to its environment and in particular to the forces that shape competition in an industry. He has always sought to understand change and the levers that attenuate success. He says in his book, *Competitive Strategy* that "industry structure has a strong influence in determining competitive rules of the game as well as the strategy potential available to the firm".

Bernard Riemann has said that "what Porter has done is to take an extremely complex environment and create a very logical order out of that complexity - which is theoretically justifiable and grounded in good economic theory, and which also makes sense to the practical manager. The terminology is a tremendous help, particularly in a multi-divisional company, because it gives common ground on which the firm's managers can stand". I agree. In Porter's terms Cost Leadership is a strategic choice that many firms can make. Managers can choose a strategic direction that leads to structural cost advantages as opposed to a strategic path towards differentiation. A company seeking pole position as cost leader in its industry will behave quite differently, employ quite different people and present itself quite differently to its customers from one that seeks to be known as unique or "differentiated".

However, "Cost Leadership" as a strategic choice is often confused with "Cost Management". No competent manager feels he has any choice about the latter! Indeed, the present enthusiasm with which many firms are substantially reducing costs and redesigning business processes, doesn't seem to me to be strategic in the Porterian sense at all. These are the actions of any manager who desires a sound and healthy company. Corporate health is <u>not</u> a strategic choice - it is a practical necessity. Every firm has to manage its costs, but not every firm will choose for a strategy of cost leadership. The latter strategy goes beyond cost management, as it requires firms to gear their businesses in all their aspects to achieving cost leadership.

The Five Forces Model
Let me return to Michael Porter's theories. Another useful model he has created for the businessman, is the notion of the five forces of competition: bargaining power of suppliers; bargaining power of buyers; the threat of new entrants; the threat of substitutes; and the rivalry between existing players (see figure 3.2).

Figure 3.2: The Five Forces Framework

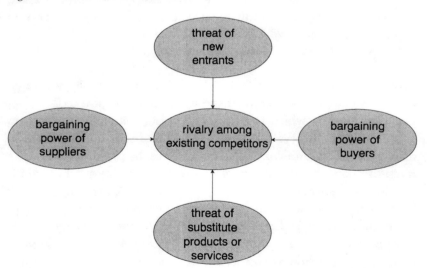

Source: Porter, 1980

The intensity of competition in any industry is related to the aggregate of these forces. And the rate of evolutionary change in an industry or, even, revolutionary change, depends on the relative strength of these five forces. With this model, once again Porter provided the manager at the business level with the terminology and the tools to analyse his own environment and exploit opportunities or at least to seek objective responses.

However, some commentators have described as arbitrary Porter's list of the forces at play. They suggest that more extensive research would have enhanced the theoretical underpinning for his model. This I cannot judge. But I would suggest to you, that those academic critics may have missed the crucial point, which businessmen did not: that the Five Forces Model works. By being so clear and so forceful, Porter enabled a generation of business managers to analyse and question more acutely their own environments and to raise the level of internal strategic debate at the business level. Most importantly, it allowed them to add value to their businesses for the benefit of all their stakeholders.

Collaborate or stand alone?

I have mentioned Porter's model for generic strategies and Porter's five forces model. May I now turn to my final point, and one which has particular interest to me in the context of a Group that has a great many autonomous operating companies around the world and, like many in the oil and gas industry, a long history of partnerships and shared endeavour.

In recent years the trend towards cross-border alliances and joint ventures has taken on the appearance of some fashionable prescriptions for corporate success. There is a premise, it seems, that, if you can just get economies of scale and lower your input costs, you will succeed. However, Porter has been quoted as saying that "this whole approach is fundamentally flawed. It misunderstands the true nature of competition. Leading companies gain success from their ability to improve and change and innovate". He goes on to say that "Some modest economies of scale may be achieved by a merger or an alliance. But you almost guarantee that companies will not be as dynamic nor as innovative as they were". This is the toll of a bell, business managers must heed.

Blindly following where fashion leads cannot ensure competitive success. Preventing the erosion or the dilution of one's distinctive competences is vitally important. "Great companies don't imitate competitors - they act differently," says Porter. Great companies stay that way, not by imitating their competitors, but by being different.

Although, like Porter, I have tended to talk mainly of tools and techniques, I agree with him when he says "No tool can remove the need for creativity in selecting the right strategy". It is a fitting point on which to close. Tools and techniques, models and modelling, vocabulary and taxonomy, are merely artefacts. Porter's great contribution at the business level has been to present these tools as transitional objects, as a means to inspire firms, large and small, to seek that "difference", to seek the competitive edge, to seek indeed, the elixir of business life.

4.

Porter on corporate strategy

Ron J.H. Meyer
Henk W.Volberda

Introduction

Many companies believe in the virtue of being active in more than one business. These firms have based their strategy of diversification on the assumption that multi-business involvement will lead to synergies that outweigh the extra costs of managing a more complex organization. *Corporate*, or *multi-business*, strategy deals with the identification and realisation of these synergies. Or as Michael Porter puts it, "corporate strategy is what makes the corporate whole add up to more than the sum of its business unit parts."

Most writers, including Porter, agree that strategizing for the corporate whole involves finding answers to two key questions, namely:

1. What businesses should the corporation be in to realize synergies? This issue is also referred to as the *composition* question (De Wit & Meyer, 1994).
2. How should this array of businesses be managed to achieve the anticipated synergies? This issue is also referred to as the *control* question.

F.A.J. van den Bosch and A.P. de Man (eds.), Perspectives on Strategy, 25-33.
© 1997 *Kluwer Academic Publishers. Printed in the Netherlands.*

The prevalent view on these issues, before Porter made his main contribution to this topic area in 1987, was the *portfolio approach* (see Haspeslagh, 1980; Henderson, 1979; Hofer & Schendel, 1977). The term portfolio entered the business vocabulary via the financial sector, where it refers to an investor's *collection of shareholdings* in different companies, purchased to spread investment risks. This basic idea was subsequently transferred to corporate strategy. Corporate headquarters was viewed as an investor with financial stakes in a number of stand-alone business units. In this conception of corporate strategy, the multi-business synergies to be realized were seen as mainly financial. Three types of financially-oriented synergies were identified:

a) *Financial Discipline.* By tough financial control at the corporate level, business managers could be instilled with a stronger measure of financial discipline, than if they had been entirely independent;
b) *Optimal Financial Resource Allocation.* By redirecting flows of cash from business units where prospects are dim ("cash cows" or "dogs"), to other business units where higher returns could be expected ("stars" or "question marks"), the corporate level could achieve a higher overall return on investment, than if the businesses had been entirely independent;
c) *Risk Spreading.* By being involved in many different, and preferably counter-cyclical businesses, a corporation could avoid "putting all the company's eggs in one basket", and thus achieve a lower aggregate level of risk, than if the businesses had been entirely independent.

To deal with the question of *composition*, a number of portfolio grids were developed, such as the Boston Consultancy Group matrix, the General Electric business screen and the Arthur D. Little matrix. All portfolio grid techniques had in common that the corporation's businesses were evaluated with regard to their strength and the attractiveness of their industry. Depending on their position on the grid, each business unit could be assigned a financially-oriented strategic mission - grow, hold or milk. Depending on the portfolio balance between mature cash generators and high potential-ROI cash users, revealed by the grid, corporate management could divest or acquire businesses to optimize the corporate composition.

With regard to the issue of *control*, since only financial linkages between the business units were emphasized, in principle each business unit could be run in isolation from the others. In other words, the complexity of corporate diversity could be managed by *disaggregation* - each business unit could be run independently, with corporate headquarters focusing on resource allocation and financial control. It should be noted that even proponents of the portfolio perspective had to admit that multiple interdependencies between business units often did exist. However, the portfolio approach offered little advice on how to manage these.

Porter's writings on corporate strategy

Porter has not written extensively on the topic of corporate strategy. This is probably because he believes that corporations do not compete, but businesses do. Therefore, he seems more fascinated by the dynamics of competition at the business level, than in the complexities of corporate level strategy. Nevertheless, he has written one article on the topic, entitled "From Competitive Advantage to Corporate Strategy", which was published in the May/June 1987 edition of *Harvard Business Review*. This article, which received the McKinsey Award for the best HBR article of the year, has had a significant impact on both corporate thinking and academic debate.

In this article Michael Porter stages a head on attack against the popular portfolio approach, since he believes that the interdependencies between the business units are the very *raison d'être* of the multi-business firm. He argues that shareholders are better at spreading investment risks than companies are, while capital markets are far better at providing financing and at instilling financial discipline. In his opinion, the value added by the corporate center of a portfolio conglomerate usually does not outweigh the extra costs and constraints, making the corporate whole less than the sum of its business unit parts. Synergy between the parts can only be achieved, Porter argues, if the corporate center strives to create and manage *value adding linkages* between the various business units. In this article he focuses on the transfer of skills and the sharing of activities as the two ways of linking the value chains of different business units.

Transfer of skills. The simplest way for business units to work together is to share knowledge and to increase each others' abilities. Since every activity in the value chain requires certain know-how, all types of skills can be transferred, ranging from logistical to service and human resource management skills. Some of this know-how is relatively easy to transmit to other units, because it can be formalized and quickly absorbed, but many skills require prolonged co-operation and concerted effort to transfer. If such *learning* creates or strengthens a business unit's competitive advantage, Porter argues that having multiple businesses within one company is justified.

Sharing of activities. Business units can go even one step further in their co-operation by linking some of their value chain activities. By bringing activities together, business units go beyond joint learning, to achieve better economies of scale and a stronger bargaining position. Here, too, Porter emphasizes that all types of value adding activities can be linked, ranging from operations to sales and technology development. Only if such *scale* advantages create or strengthen a business unit's competitive position, does Porter believe that there is value in having more than one business in a company.

So, when confronted with the *composition* question, Porter argues that a corporation should only select those businesses that have good skill transfer and activity sharing potential. Only business units that offer such synergies will make the corporation better off. Porter refers to this argument as the *better-off test* for determining the corporation's composition. It is one of three simple tests that he offers to screen each potential addition to the corporation's array of businesses. According to Porter, to truly create shareholder value, each diversification move should pass:

- *The attractiveness test*. The industries chosen for diversification must be structurally attractive or capable of being made attractive;
- *The cost of entry test*. The cost of entry must not capitalize all future profits.
- *The better-off test*. The new unit must gain competitive advantage from its link with the corporation or vice versa;

Furthermore, Porter suggests that it might be useful for a multi-business company to develop a *corporate theme*. Such a theme, like NEC's emphasis on computers and communication equipment (C&C), focuses a company's diversification efforts and enlarges the possibility that skill transfer and activity sharing can be achieved.

While outspoken on the topic of composition, Porter is almost silent with regard to the issue of control. He recognizes that managing the chosen array of businesses is a challenging task, yet he does not concern himself with these organizationally-oriented issues. Neither the co-ordination between business units to achieve skill transfer and activity sharing, nor the role of the corporate center are dealt with at any length.

Porter's contribution to corporate strategy thinking

Maybe the best way to evaluate Michael Porter's contribution to the subject of corporate strategy is to apply his ideas to himself. After all, the topic of business strategy has been Porter's "core business" throughout the years, while his writings on corporate strategy could be viewed as a diversification move. The obvious question that should be asked, therefore, is whether Porter's venture into the related field of corporate strategy passes all three diversification tests:

- *The attractiveness test*. It is unnecessary to argue that in a world economy populated by so many multi-business firms, the topic of corporate strategy is extremely important. What made the subject so interesting for Porter was the relatively underdeveloped state of corporate strategy theory at the time he wrote his article in 1987. Although serious doubts had been raised about the portfolio approach, both in theory (e.g. Prahalad & Bettis, 1986) and in practice ("back to the core"), an alternative approach still needed to emerge. Porter's article made a valuable *contribution to this transition* from portfolio thinking to a synergy-oriented view of the multi-business firm.

- *The cost of entry test*: Entering the field of corporate strategy was relatively easy for Porter - no major acquisition was needed, it was all achievable through internal growth. This was because his business strategy philosophy could easily be extended to the corporate level. In Porter's view, competition is rooted within an industry's structure and a business strategy should focus on creating and sustaining a competitive advantage for the business unit within its industry. When applied to the corporate level, this perspective leads to the conclusion that corporate strategy should concern itself with improving each business's competitive position. In other words, the key issue of corporate strategy is not financial control and risk spreading, but increasing business units' long term competitiveness. As such, Porter's article has made a valuable *contribution to defining the focus* of corporate strategy.

- *The better-off test*: Porter's contribution to shifting the emphasis of corporate strategy toward "synergy" and "competitive advantage" has definitely left the field much better off. In this context it should be noted that a part of Porter's strength has been his eagerness to go beyond talking about the general concepts of synergy and competitive advantage, by trying to pin down where these synergies can be realized that enhance competitive advantage. To achieve this, he "transfers a skill" from his business strategy writings - the "value chain" methodology - and applies it within the corporate strategy setting. As such, Porter has made a valuable *contribution to the operationalization* of the concept of synergy.

On the whole, it can be concluded that Michael Porter has made a number of useful contributions to the field of corporate strategy. His article "From Competitive Advantage to Corporate Strategy" is often cited, although his position within the field is not as prominent as it is on the topic of business strategy.

Criticisms of Porter's perspective on corporate strategy

Beside compliments there have also been a number of criticisms of Porter's ideas, either directly or indirectly. It is noteworthy that hardly any of these criticisms are based on a fundamental disagreement with Porter's point of view. Rather, the broad thrust of these critiques is that he does not go far enough, or that his concepts need further clarification. The most important points brought forward are the following:

Premature dismissal of the portfolio approach. Porter brushes aside financially-oriented portfolios, because he believes that they do not create shareholder value - arguing that investors can spread their own risk and capital markets are far better at providing finance. However, there has been one significant defence of the portfolio approach. Goold and Campbell (1987) argue that there are a few circumstances under which a portfolio approach (which they call *financial control style*) can be preferable - when managing an array of relatively simple, mature, stand alone businesses, which require a strict focus on efficiency and low cost (e.g. Hanson and Grand Met). In this type of a situation financial discipline is a key competitive advantage. A "lean and mean" corporate center can often add value by using tough financial control to keep costs down. Therefore, Goold and Campbell argue that the portfolio approach should remain in view as an alternative to Porter's ideas if certain conditions are met.

Lack of attention for organizational issues. A second comment is that Porter only speaks of potential synergies, but does not concern himself with the question how they can be realized within the organization. In other words, Porter writes about the "why" of diversification, but not about the "how". Yet, determining how to manage the organizational complexity caused by the integration of divers company parts is a central issue within corporate strategy. How can skills be transferred and how can activities be shared are obvious questions, that Porter does not touch on.

Difficulty in operationalizing the better-off test. A third comment on Porter's article is that the better-off test sounds simple in theory, but is extremely difficult to use in practice (Goold & Campbell, 1991). It is an appealing guide-line to only diversify into those businesses that will improve their competitive advantage by their link to the corporation, but in reality it is often difficult to determine in advance which linkages will actually add value. The possible synergies coming from the transfer of skills and the sharing of activities are not something that can be easily estimated up front. Especially in the case of a potential acquisition, it is difficult to judge what the possible synergies are and to forecast whether the possible synergies can be realized or not (Prahalad & Bettis, 1986). This means that more attention must be paid to operationalizing the better-off test - what must management focus on to estimate synergy opportunities? Alternatively, the whole idea of screening diversification moves might need to be dropped, settling instead to evaluate the success of diversification efforts after they have been effectuated. In other words, an ex-post test might make more sense than an ex-ante one.

Need for a "best-off" test. Goold and Campbell further question whether "better-off" is the correct diversification evaluation criterion. They believe that a parent company should not only add value to a new business unit and thus make them better-off, but should add *more* value than any other potential parent. Goold and Campbell argue that parent companies should ask themselves whether they offer the best potential synergies to a subsidiary. The corporation should only retain or acquire a business if they have such a *parenting advantage*.

Unclearly defined concept of corporate theme. A number of writers has commented that Porter's remarks about a "corporate theme" are rather open ended. Porter suggests that a good corporate theme can focus organizational efforts and can enlarge the possibilities for the transfer of skills and the sharing of activities. However, what is a good corporate theme and how can a company create one? Much of the literature on corporate strategy after 1987 has dealt with this topic - how can corporations be built around a common core? The most significant development has been the avalanche of attention for the concepts of *core competences* (Prahalad and Hamel, 1990) and *core capabilities* (Stalk, Evans and Shulman, 1992). These authors believe that Porter's focus on linking the value chains of independent business units does not go far enough. In their perspective, the corporation should not be viewed as a *chain*, with separate business units rings that have been linked together. Rather, the corporation should be compared with a *tree*, where all business unit branches stem from the same trunk and roots, consisting of core competences, core capabilities and/or core products. Such a conception of the corporation has led may researchers to conclude that competition does not only take place at the business level (within industries), but also at the corporate level (across industries). Entire corporations compete against other corporations in their ability to continually learn new capabilities - each industry in which these capabilities are applied is but one battlefield in the much broader war (Prahalad and Hamel, 1990). This is, however, quite a departure from Porter's premises that corporations do not compete, but businesses do.

Conclusion
As stated earlier, Porter has primarily contributed to the topic of corporate strategy by focusing attention on the issue of multi-business synergy and by making concrete where synergies can be realized. Since the publication of his article in 1987, researchers and writers in this field have further explored the origins and forms of corporate synergy. In particular, the organizational processes of creating and sustaining multi-business synergies have become more central. Topics such as developing core competences, managing intracorporate knowledge sharing, post-acquisition integration management and the role of the corporate center are currently high on the research agenda. However, in most of these corporate strategy research fields Porter is not an active participant.

While no longer at the forefront of corporate strategy research, Porter's ideas still find wide-spread acceptance and application in the business world. The fundamental notion that corporations must add more value to businesses than the stock markets can, is currently widely-held. Conglomerates based on the portfolio approach to corporate strategy have largely fallen into disrespect and multi-business firms have increasingly refocused themselves on a core of linked businesses. Porter's recognition, analysis and promotion of this trend has been an important contribution to the restructuring of many diversified companies. And as can be seen in the following chapter by the former co-chairman of Unilever, the transition from conglomerates based on the portfolio approach to focused corporations transferring skills and sharing activities has been a significant step in the evolution of the multi-business firm.

References

De Wit, B., and R. Meyer (1994), *Strategy - Process, Content, Context: An International Perspective*, St. Paul, Minn.: West.

Goold, M., and A. Campbell (1987), "Many Best Ways to make Strategy", *Harvard Business Review*, nr. 6, pp. 70-76.

Goold, M., and A. Campbell (1991), "Brief Case: From Corporate Strategy to Parenting Advantage", *Long Range Planning*, February, pp. 115-117.

Haspeslagh, P. (1982), "Portfolio Planning: Uses and Limits", *Harvard Business Review*, January/February, pp. 58-73.

Henderson, B.D. (1979), *On Corporate Strategy*, Cambridge, MA: Abt Books.

Hofer, C.W., and D.E. Schendel, *Strategy Formulation: Analytical Concepts*, St. Paul: West, pp. 30-34.

Porter, M. E. (1987), "From Competitive Advantage to Corporate Strategy", *Harvard Business Review*, May/June, pp. 43-59.

Prahalad, C.K., and R.A. Bettis (1986), "The Dominant Logic: A New Linkage Between Diversity and Performance", *Strategic Management Journal*, November/December, pp. 485-501.

Prahalad, C.K., and G. Hamel (1990), "The Core Competence of the Corporation", *Harvard Business Review*, May/June, pp. 79-91.

Stalk, G., P. Evans and L.E. Shulman (1992), "Competing on Capabilities: The New Rules of Corporate Strategy", *Harvard Business Review*, March/April, pp. 57-69.

5.

Corporate strategy from a Unilever perspective

F.A. Maljers (Professor of Strategic Management and former co-chairman of Unilever)

"Corporate strategy concerns two different questions: what businesses the corporation should be in and how the corporate office should manage the array of business units. Corporate strategy is what makes the corporate whole add up to more than the sum of its business unit parts (Porter, 1987)."

Introduction

Business strategy in the nineties would not be the same without Porter's great contribution, which combines an in-depth knowledge of industry with a clear insight in the general factors underlying the realities of business. The intention of this article is to specify the way in which Porter's thinking relates to the corporate strategy of a large multinational, multi product company, namely Unilever.

First, the history of Unilever's corporate strategy will be considered in more detail. This historical review clearly demonstrates how Unilever initially increased its number of businesses and how the company lacked coherence. Recognizing these past diversification efforts, this article will show how Unilever decided what businesses the

F.A.J. van den Bosch and A.P. de Man (eds.), Perspectives on Strategy, 35-43.
© 1997 *Kluwer Academic Publishers. Printed in the Netherlands.*

corporation should be in to realize synergies. By considering product areas as well as geographical dimensions, the corporate centre identified strategic priorities for corporate synergies. In addition to the composition of Unilever's set of businesses, this article will deal with the control question, that is, how this array of businesses should be managed and what the specific roles of corporate and divisional management in this process should be. To facilitate the transition from conglomerate to a focused corporation, Unilever disposed of a number of businesses acquired numerous others and initiated large-scale restructuring programs (Maljers, 1992). Instead of a portfolio concept of strategy with only financial synergies, Unilever created synergies in terms of transferring skills and sharing of activities. The article concludes with how corporations can maintain these synergies, as well as explore new synergies.

Unilever's corporate strategy in perspective: the limits of a portfolio strategy
In its 63 years of existence, Unilever had to struggle with the tensions between, on the one hand, growth by *diversification* and, on the other hand, *synergies* by searching for related businesses. Nowadays, Unilever operates in four industries: foods, detergents, personal care products, and selected specialty chemicals. All of these product groups have in some shape or form been part of Unilever since 1930, when the company was created as the result of the merger of a Dutch food group and a British soap company.

The two decades following World War II were used to rebuild and consolidate these businesses but this changed during the late sixties and the seventies. Strategic thinking of the day favoured the creation of widely-spread conglomerates and Unilever, too, followed the prevailing fashion and diversified into transport, packaging, agribusiness and some even more improbable activities like wallpaper and bicycle wholesaling.

In the mid eighties corporate management began to feel somewhat uneasy about the lack of coherence of these activities and decided to review systematically Unilever's product range. They concluded that, if they wanted to be successful in an increasingly competitive world, they would have to focus on the areas where they had proven strength and a high level of professionalism. In this way they could meet the Clausewitz criterium - operate in markets where you can set the rules, not where you have to follow the rules set by others. That, not surprisingly, brought Unilever basically back to the core areas of the founding fathers.

In search of a corporate theme

In line with Michael Porter's view on the multi-business firm (1980, 1985), Unilever believes that there are advantages in having a number of different but related businesses in one corporation. However, this only makes sense if there are common elements to create cohesion between the various parts or what Porter (1987) calls a *'Corporate Theme'*. If the existence of the corporation does not clearly add value to the individual parts, it might be preferable to split the company into its major components. This would also give a clearer choice to investors, as the recent examples of ICI, ITT, and AT&T make clear.

This is very much in line with Porter's view when he expresses serious doubts about the *portfolio approach* to corporate management as a way to organize and manage a multi-product firm. In defining the strategy for a company an important first step is to identify both the chosen product areas and the geographical ambitions.

Identifying product areas

The strategic selection of the product areas should be based, above all, on Porter's *better-off test*, that is, an audit for evaluating the potential internal synergies between the various parts of the total range. This requires a thorough and sometimes painful analysis of the strengths and, equally important, the weaknesses of the corporation. The strengths can, for instance, lie in a particular science base that is multi-applicable such as the behaviour of emulsions. The common element can also be in functional skills such as marketing. In searching for coherence, one has to be aware that sometimes internal synergies fail to emerge where they are expected, while they may exist in products where they are not so obvious. There is more in common, technologically, between margarine and lipstick than most people think, to give just one example.

Besides the better-off test for realizing synergies between product areas, the choice of a single product area should be based on an analysis of the *attractiveness of the industry* chosen and the *cost of entry*. The cost of entry must not capitalize all the future profits. In this connection, Porter's (1980) concepts like 'barriers to entry', 'rivalry among existing firms' and 'bargaining power of suppliers and buyers' can play an important role. It is sufficient to say here that the identification of areas for core activities can benefit enormously from the use of Porter's five forces framework.

In addition, the concept of sustainability is essential for Unilever's survival. The industries chosen for diversification must be structurally attractive or capable of being made attractive. A thorough analysis of the developments expected in the markets in which Unilever operates is a condition to minimize the dangers of what Porter calls erosion by competitor behaviour or 'industry evolution'. This is tough because a company tries to hit a moving target. Especially 'industry evolution' can be a major threat because discontinuities can change markets very rapidly. These discontinuities can be technological, such as the rise of the Personal Computer, or political, the fall of Marxism, or in the competitive environment, for instance the aggressive acquisition strategy of Philip Morris in the foods industry. The real skill is not only to identify but, above all, to be able to anticipate new trends. Unilever needs to develop superior industry foresight (Prahalad & Hamel, 1990). Only then can one prepare for the new developments and benefit from them. Corporate management realizes that this is far from easy, but it is a basic skill required for a successful entrepreneur.

Identifying geographical areas
Besides choosing product areas, Unilever had to take into account the second strategic dimension, the geographical spread of the corporation. Strategic considerations at this moment in time are influenced by the many exciting new opportunities such as the opening up of more markets than ever before. In the eighties we saw the Triad concept, which seemed at that time all that mattered. The era of Post-Marxism in Central Europe and the former Soviet Union and the economic opening of China, seem to have changed all that. This is not surprising because even enthusiastic Triadists may find it difficult to resist the temptation of the Chinese market with 1.2 billion consumers and a 10% economic growth, even though there are still risks. Should Unilever therefore change its selection criteria dramatically, follow current fashion and go global without further ado? In this connection, the Economist magazine wrote "Think Global, - then think again". This development may illustrate the danger of a dogmatic approach to business strategy. However, the new country opportunities are, of course, only one aspect of the new geography. Equally important are the new regional economic groupings. The most important is still the

economic dimension of the European Union, generally known as the Single European Market. This will hopefully be followed by NAFTA and other free trade areas elsewhere in the not too distant future. All the developments summarised, and many more, mean that identifying strategic priorities currently has a much more important geographical dimension than ten, or even five years ago.

The managerial question of control: integration of dispersed activities

Besides choosing what businesses, in terms of product and geographical dimensions, Unilever should be in, an important managerial issue is how this array of businesses has to be managed to achieve the anticipated synergies. Going back to the objective of formulating a corporate strategy, one should not forget that Unilever has to allocate its scarce resources, notably management and money, to those activities where they will add most to shareholder value. At this moment the opportunities in new countries and new regional groups are such, that even a large multi-product corporation has to exercise some control and watch out for too much product- diversification. This managerial challenge of control relates to the question in which parts of the value system the corporation wants to be present and what the specific roles of corporate and divisional management in this process should be.

The role of corporate and divisional management

An important question regarding this question of control is the extent to which the identification of core product areas and geographical areas is a task and a responsibility for the corporate level and where and when divisional management should take over. For instance, in how far should corporate management be involved in identifying where in the large food industry Unilever should be primarily investing? As mentioned before, one of the main corporate priorities is food, representing slightly more than half of Unilever's present turnover. In order to realize synergies, choosing core product areas must be a managerial task of corporate management. For the selection of the food sub-groups Unilever uses the same selection criteria as summarised above for the total product range. To give an example, Unilever is the largest tea company in the world and continues to build on its strength with new products. The temptation is great to look at the opportunities in coffee, after all an adjacent area. However, the 'extended rivalry' in the coffee market is such that corporate management always reaches the same conclusion - this is not attractive for us.

Each board of a corporation has to decide how specific it wants to be in establishing corporate priority-groups or sub-groups. Having established in how far the corporate level wants to define the strategic areas, the more detailed priority setting should then be left to the managements of the individual Product Groups. Unilever has decided, for instance, that tea in all forms has a very high corporate priority but leaves the decision how much of the scarce marketing resources the tea group should allocate to hot tea and how much to iced tea, for instance, to the directly responsible management.

Control over activities in the value chain
In addition to the managerial tasks regarding the product dimension and geography, management has to decide on those parts in the total production chain for given products in which the corporation wants to be present. This raises issues such as how far a company wants to go upstream or downstream in a certain industry and also which services it wants to have in house and which should be supplied by others. This is at the moment a much discussed issue in many companies, where the traditional inclination toward control over all services and processes is being replaced by an increasing tendency to rely on third parties and to privatise parts of the traditional activities. Here again, the determinant should be how the company makes best use of its resources. This is, again, an important area where Porter (1985) has developed some interesting ideas. He speaks of the *value chain* and bases his analysis on activities. These are divided into primary activities and support activities. It is very tempting to comment on Porter's very important and interesting work in this field, but in this contribution we will limit ourselves to one comment. A company has to define and retain those activities which are absolutely essential to give it a sustainable competitive advantage. This may sound obvious, but there is sometimes a temptation to accept low cost alternatives, without fully realising the intangible values that can be lost. Application of the value chain concept can be a great help in corporate strategic thinking, but has to take account of many aspects. It is an area where we may have to accept intuition as a valuable addition to quantification. The basis of every strategic combination of activities in a corporation is, as already said, the existence of internal synergies.

Maintaining and developing synergies

How can a multi-business firm like Unilever maximally exploit and maintain existing synergies and at the same time explore new potential synergies? In analyzing this question, Porter (1987) identified four concepts of corporate strategy that have been put into practice: portfolio management, restructuring, transferring skills, and sharing activities. While the concepts are not always mutually exclusive, each rests on a different mechanism by which the corporation creates shareholder value and each requires the diversified company to manage and organize itself in a different way. The first two require no connections among business units, while the second two depend on them. In its corporate strategy, Unilever has made a shift from a predominantly portfolio concept towards a transferring skills concept and even sharing of activities concept. This shift will be discussed below.

Transfer of skills

The transfer of skills between business units in the diversified company is the basis for one concept. While each business unit has a separate value chain, knowledge about how to perform activities is transferred among the units. Transfer of skills between countries and regions seems an easy task when looked at from a distance but requires in practice the right management culture and a well-designed organisation structure. A number of issues have to be solved, such as the often-discussed balance between centralisation and delegation. Centralisation can improve a rapid exchange of experience, it can in other words lead to a faster descent along the learning curve. However, bureaucracy, the fearsome companion of centralisation, can lead to petrified structures that stifle creativity in the operating units. The balance of advantages and disadvantages has to be watched carefully and occasional organisational shake-ups may be required to encourage the head office staff to remain flexible.

Unilever's management culture has traditionally always encouraged the use of the informal organisation which Unilever, like most companies, has. That Unilever's informal structure is so important and effective is more by accident than by design and is basically a by-product of a very intensive program of training, attachments and job rotation, which creates this formidable network. "Transfer of skills" benefits enormously from this informal exchange of information, which has the added advantage that it acts in practice as a competitive force to the head office experts and, like most forms of competition, improves the quality of both.

Transferring skills between Product Groups poses different issues. The most important aspect is often technology. Fat science, for instance can be applied, in skin cream, in soap making, in frying fat, in oleo-chemicals, in margarine, in ice cream, in bakery materials and many other of our products. The increasing degree of scientific specialisation, necessary to improve Unilever's products requires major expenditure on Research and Development. One could even say that economies of scale in R&D are an important reason for the existence of large companies. The responsibility to use the existing science base as broadly as possible is shared in Unilever between the Research Director and the Product Groups. However, whilst Unilever has made much progress in the last decade in integrating science in the business, the company still has some way to go. A major issue is that the prediction of consumer behaviour over a longer period becomes notoriously difficult once corporate management wants to go beyond the often rather platitudinous general trends often mentioned in popular publications.

Sharing of activities

According to Porter (1987), the ability to share activities is a potent basis for corporate strategy because sharing often enhances competitive advantage by lowering cost or raising differentiation. Sharing of activities can be achieved through the use of a Central Service or by a system of direct sharing between operating units. On the corporate central level there are a number of obvious examples of common expertise. Above we just mentioned technology but there are other areas such as the use of financial strength, the fiscal expertise and Management Development. As a manufacturer of fast moving consumer goods Unilever sees marketing as one of its central skills and has a group of people in the head office that acts as a clearing house for expertise in advertising, market research and sales management. Much sharing of activities takes place on the national level, especially outside Europe and North America. In countries like Chile or Nigeria or Thailand Unilever has one organisation handling the whole product range. And in countries where Unilever has more than one operating unit, there is close contact on issues of common interest such as trade relations or labelling legislation. At the regional level there is also quite a bit of sharing of activities. To give some illustrations, on the regional level Unilever has a bakery expert in Jakarta serving South East Asia and in São Paulo Unilever has a logistics expert for South America.

Conclusion

In this contribution it was demonstrated in which way a number of Porter's ideas are applied in Unilever such as the five forces model, the value chain and most importantly Porter's concepts of corporate strategy. While the portfolio approach of strategic management has succeeded under certain circumstances, today the transferring of skills and sharing of activities make more sense. Let us conclude by expressing our admiration for the contribution that Michael Porter has made to strategic thinking. He has certainly handed Unilever tools that will help the corporation to further improve business performance.

References

Maljers, F.A. (1992), "Inside Unilever: The Evolving Transnational Company", *Harvard Business Review*, Sept./Oct., pp. 46-51.

Porter, M.E. (1980), *Competitive Strategy: Techniques for Analyzing Industries and Competitors*, New York: Free Press.

Porter, M.E. (1985), *Competitive Advantage: Creating and Sustaining Superior Advantage*, New York: Free Press.

Porter, M.E. (1987), "From Competitive Advantage to Corporate Strategy", *Harvard Business Review*, May/June, pp. 43-59.

Prahalad, C.K., and G. Hamel (1990), "The Core Competence of the Corporation", *Harvard Business Review*, Vol. 68, pp. 79-91.

6.

Porter on national and regional

competitive advantage

Ard-Pieter de Man, Frans van den Bosch, Tom Elfring

Introduction: approaches to competitiveness
In the last decade, the issue of competitiveness has captured an
important position on the agenda of politicians and policymakers. The
growing strength of Asian firms on the world market has been debated
at some length in both the USA and in Europe. In the USA the focus of
the debate was on the trade deficit and the weak performance of
American firms compared to their Japanese competitors. In the
European countries competitiveness became a buzzword in the
discussions about rising unemployment. An increase in
competitiveness was not only seen as a remedy against the lay-offs in
mature industries but was believed to spur growth rates in new high-
tech sectors as well.

These discussions about competitiveness can be divided into three
distinct schools of inquiry (Nelson, 1991). The first school has the
individual firm as the unit of analysis. These studies stress that the
determining factors of competitiveness reside within the firm. In this
view the existence and survival of a firm is about combining difficult to
imitate resources in a coherent way. A failure to achieve that has,

F.A.J. van den Bosch and A.P. de Man (eds.), Perspectives on Strategy, 45-59.
© *1997 Kluwer Academic Publishers. Printed in the Netherlands.*

according to the authors working in this tradition, to do with the internal side of the firm. In the USA for example, the discussion focused on the short time horizon of American companies, compared to European and Japanese firms. The success of some of the latter companies can be traced back to their stamina and long-term investments in marketing, technology and human capital (Chandler, 1990). American firms seem to retreat from industries with low rates of return fairly swiftly, they don't want to wait for better times. Instead of following these stop-and-go strategies, American firms should show more commitment according to this school of research. It is argued that a company must commit itself to develop a set of capabilities superior to its competitors in order to create a competitive advantage (Ghemawat, 1991).

American firms might lack commitment, Dutch firms seem to be overly committed to mature industries. They lack the capability to innovate and shift from the mature mass production sectors to niche markets with customized high value-added products (Metze, 1990; Jacobs, et al., 1990). Similar to this is the analysis that American firms are still applying old style mass-production methods, while markets demand a more flexible manufacturing approach (Dertouzos, et al., 1989). On a general level the problem that the business environment has changed while firms have not, applies to some European firms as well. In Europe many companies have to adjust to more competitive circumstances, as a result of the breakdown of national borders, cartels and monopolies.

Quite opposite to the inside-out perspective of the first school, the literature in the second and third school are driven by an outside-in approach. The second school of writings can be labelled as the industrial policy debate. The industry is the unit of analysis, and the main thrust of this type of literature is how the government can shape the industry environment in order to foster the growth, profitability and competitiveness of the firms within that industry. Different roles of the government can be distinguished. The government can play a leading role in guiding and directing industrial activities. The prime example is the MITI in Japan. However, usually the government's involvement is less farreaching. Often it is about the creation of mechanisms to coordinate, stimulate or support certain activities, for example research and development or high-tech industries. The least active role of the government is the one of facilitator: creating conditions for companies to work together, establish networks or ease the diffusion of innovations are examples of this.

The third school of studies deals with the impact of the macro-environment on the competitiveness of the business community. This is a somewhat diverse group. It ranges from the negative impact of the low saving rate and limited public education on competitiveness in the United States to the detrimental effects of high tax rates and high wages costs in Europe on its competitiveness. In short, in this school macro variables are seen as the key to good performance. The three schools are summarized in table 6.1.

Table 6.1: Three traditions of research into competitiveness identified by Nelson

	Unit of analysis	**Key to competitiveness**
First school	firm	superior management
Second school	industry	industrial policy
Third school	macro-economic conditions	low interest rates, taxes, wages etc.

These three schools of writings about the issue of competitiveness have developed more or less independently. There have been only limited efforts to integrate those three distinct strands of reasoning. As a result opportunities for new insights were missed. In this chapter we will position the contribution of Porter as an effort to integrate those three separate schools of thought into his diamond framework. This framework allows us to analyze the influence of the macro-environment on firm behaviour in industries.

A puzzle
After having analyzed the role of industry structure (Porter, 1980) and the value chain (Porter, 1985), Porter was confronted with a *puzzle*. He observed that competitive advantage in particular industries is often concentrated in a certain country, often with several successful competitors based in the same region. How to explain this phenomenon? This puzzle stimulated Porter to accept a richer view of the role of the business environment. This view emerged from his analysis of the causes of international competitive success of firms as

described in his thought provoking book of 1990: *The Competitive Advantage of Nations.*

Subject of the competitive advantage of nations book

As pointed out above, in the eighties the question arose: Why do some nations succeed and others fail in international competition? According to Porter, this is the wrong question. In keeping with other critics of the concept of national competitiveness (e.g. Krugman, 1994), Porter claims that not nations compete, but firms do within internationalizing industries. Hence, Porter proposes as a research question to look for determinants in the national business environment that can explain why in some countries firms in particular industries are more successful than those in other nations. This way of approaching the international competitiveness of firms was quite novel. The various aspects of this key question are illustrated in table 6.2. As can be seen from this table concepts like the home base of international firms, the capacity to improve (Porter likes the word 'upgrading') and to innovate are connected with this research question. The home base is defined as the nation in which the essential competitive advantages of the firm are created and maintained. Other activities can be performed in a variety of other nations. Upgrading is described as the process of improving the value chain in such a way that more sophisticated types of competitive advantage come into being. These can for example employ higher levels of skills and technology or emerge from close working relationships with suppliers.

Table 6.2: Various aspects of the key research question posed in Porter's book The Competitive Advantage of Nations (1990)

a) What is the role played by a nation's economic environment, institution, and policies in shaping the competitive success of firms in particular industries?
b) Why does a nation become the home base for successful international competitors in an industry?
c) Why and how do multinationals from a particular nation develop unique skills and know-how in particular industries?
d) How does a nation provide an environment in which its firms are able to improve and innovate faster than foreign rivals in a particular industry?

Source: based on Porter (1990, chapter 1).

Aim and approach

Porter's aim is quite clearly stated as follows: "My aim is to help firms and governments, who must act, choose better strategies and make informed allocation of national resources" (p. 30). His message to managers of firms is clear as well: "what I have found is that firms will not ultimately succeed unless they base their strategies on improvement and innovation, a willingness to compete, and a realistic understanding of their national environment and how to improve it. The view that globalization eliminates the importance of the home base rests on false premises, as does the alluring strategy of avoiding competition." (p. 30). These clear recommendations are based on a very thoroughly performed research project in which ten important trading countries (a.o. USA, UK, Japan, Germany, Italy) are investigated regarding internationally successful industries at three points in time: 1971, 1978 and 1985. Porter analyzed the patterns of these successful industries in each country over time and paid special attention to the relationships among a nation's competitive industries: the so called clusters, which are industries connected through vertical and horizontal relationships. The research results in a framework which describes the determinants of competitiveness: the diamond.

The diamond framework

The diamond framework consists of four determinants and two additional variables, together forming a mutually interacting system (see figure 6.1). Factor conditions deal with a nation's position in factors of production, such as skilled labour and knowledge resources. Of special importance are the advanced and specialized factors. These factors are difficult to procure in global markets and provide a sustainable basis for competitive advantage. Porter gives interesting examples of how competitive advantage can grow out of a disadvantage in some factors. In this connection he points at the Dutch cut flower industry (also see chapter 7), by far the world leader in this industry, despite Holland's relatively "cold and grey climate". Regarding the second determinant of demand conditions, three attributes are distinguished. The most important attributes of home demand are those that in particular create initial and ongoing incentives for investment and innovation. In this connection, demanding local buyers, consumer needs that anticipate those of other nations and early saturation of the home market are very important. The third determinant, related and supporting industries, deals with the presence and absence in the national environment of internationally competitive related and supporting industries. For example, internationally competitive semiconductors and software industries have an important impact on many other industries. Related industries create the possibility of sharing activities in value chains with respect to for example manufacturing and distribution. Of the fourth determinant especially domestic rivalry is important. Porter states: "Among the strongest empirical findings from our research is the association between vigorous domestic rivalry and the creation and persistence of competitive advantage in an industry" (p. 117). Porter even claims that domestic rivalry is more important than international competition, especially when it leads to pressure on domestic firms to improve and to innovate in ways that upgrade their competitive advantage. In particular, geographic concentration of domestic rivals creates a fertile environment for innovations. We will elaborate on this aspect below when discussing the subject of regions and cities as "diamonds".

Figure 1: The diamond framework

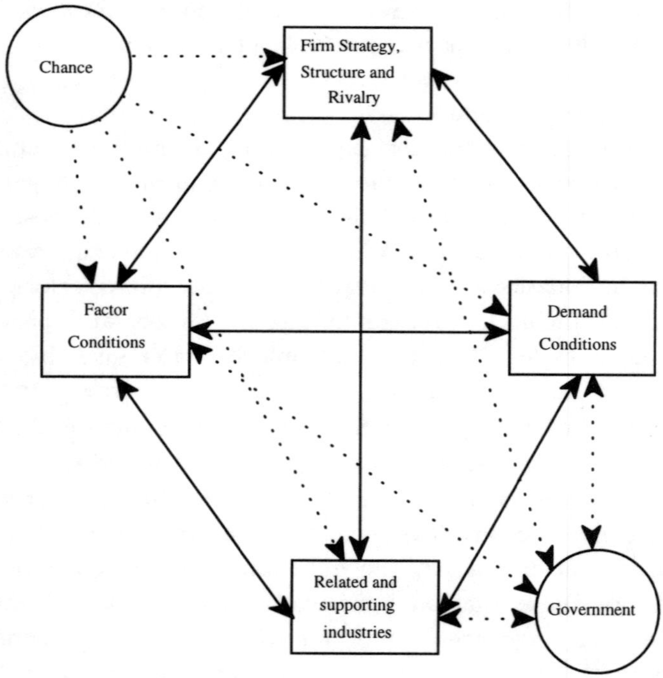

Source: Porter (1990)

The two additional variables in the diamond framework are chance and government. Chance events are considered to be exogenous factors, that is outside the power of firms to influence. Examples are significant shifts of exchange rates and political decisions by foreign governments. The second additional variable concerns the role of government in creating international competitiveness. According to Porter, government's true role in national competitive advantage is in influencing the four already distinguished determinants. This influence can be either positive or negative. An example of a positive influence is the early recognition of facsimile documents as legal documents by the Japanese government, which stimulated early demand for facsimile equipment. An example of a negative influence is the highly restrictive Italian regulation of local financial markets, leading to a disadvantage for Italian financial institutions in international competition. Porter does not deny the influence of the government on national competitive advantage, but states that its role is inevitably partial: the government lacks the power to create national competitive advantage directly by itself.

The core of competitiveness therefore lies at the firm level. That is why Porter's analysis does not remain at the national level, but pays considerable attention to the upgrading strategies of firms as well. Not only the internal organization of firms is important in this regard, but also the way in which firms stimulate the diamond surrounding them, for instance by transferring knowledge to customers and suppliers. In other words, Nelson's (1991) first school of studies as discussed in the introduction, is represented in the diamond framework as well.

The diamond framework as a dynamic system
Porter's diamond framework is not a static framework. On the contrary, the effect of one determinant depends on the development of and interaction with the other determinants (see figure 1). The determinants reinforce each other and as this mutual reinforcement proceeds, the contribution of each determinant to national competitive advantage becomes blurred. However, two elements play a key role in making the diamond a really dynamic self-reinforcing system.

These elements are domestic rivalry and geographic industry concentration. Domestic rivalry in particular stimulates the upgrading of the diamond while geographic concentration especially magnifies the interactions within the diamond. These geographic industry concentrations give rise to groups of connected industries, the so-called *clusters*. Porter observed that successful industries are usually linked through vertical links, that is buyer/supplier relationships, and/or through horizontal links, for example common demanding customers or distribution channels. These vertical and horizontal links provide mechanisms for the exchange and flow of information among buyers, suppliers and related industries. If these links do not reduce active rivalry, the conditions for competitive advantage in the cluster are favourable. The emergence of these clusters can be explained by the diamond framework as for example competitive supplier industries stimulate the emergence and competitiveness of downstream industries. The competitiveness of an industry becomes dependent on the competitiveness of other related and supporting industries as well. This means in fact that national competitive advantage resides as much at the level of the cluster as it does in individual industries.

Regions and cities as diamonds

On the basis of his extensive research Porter concludes that: "Competitors in many internationally successful industries, and often entire clusters of industries, are often located in a single town or region within a nation." (p. 154). Porter observed that cities and regions can contain a remarkable concentration of rivals, customers and suppliers leading to not only efficiencies and specialization, but to concentration of information and visibility of competitor behavior as well. Porter's examples of these geographic concentrations in Germany are the steel industry around Dortmunt, Essen and Düsseldorf, the machine tool industry in Stuttgart and the cutlery industry in Solingen. Basel is the home base for the Swiss pharmaceutical giants. British auctioneers are "all within a few blocks in London".

The question rises whether this wellknown empirical phenomenon can be explained by the diamond framework. Although this diamond framework is originally developed for and applied at the level of the national environment, Porter claims that it can be applied successfully at the regional and city level as well: "Indeed, the reasons why a particular city or region is successful in a particular industry are captured by the same considerations embodied in the 'diamond'" (p. 158). Porter elaborated this line of reasoning even further by investigating the competitive advantage of the inner city.

In a Harvard Business Review Article published May 1995, Porter pays attention to this subject using the diamond framework and criticising the existing approaches, labelled by him as "social models", in which the government's role is dominant. In accordance with his diamond framework in which the government's role in creating a competitive advantage is indirect, Porter criticises the leading role of the government in the existing approaches to city development. Moreover, normally inner cities are considered in isolation from their surrounding urban areas and regional economy. On the basis of his diamond framework, Porter stresses the necessity of integrating the inner city with the regional economy.

By firstly identifying the main competitive advantages of the inner city (like its strategic location and local market demand), insight can be gained into possibilities for further development. Secondly, when the real disadvantages of the inner city like the high cost of building space and security are addressed, there is a basis for business development in the inner city. The private sector should have the leading role in that, and not the government. This brief sketch of the application of Porter's diamond framework at the inner city level clearly shows a lot of valuable clues for strategy formation of firms already present in inner cities or of those considering such a location.

An evaluation of Porter's contribution to the study of competitiveness

Evaluating Porter's contribution to our understanding of national and regional competitive advantage, it must be remarked that first of all Porter's approach is used in practice by various governments. The next two chapters will give some examples of this in the Netherlands and the Rotterdam region. So far the influence of Porter's work on the business community seems to be less farreaching, even though the number of firms which actively upgrade their diamonds appears to be augmenting.

A question raised in the debate surrounding Porter's book is whether his view is completely new. Of course it is not: the importance of networks for innovation for example had been established before Porter published his research results. This underscores how well-grounded Porter's research is in theory. In addition, Porter's work is grounded in practice as well. It is this combination of theory and practice which emanated in a practical method for studying national competitiveness. This combination of theory, practice and tools forms the core of Porter's innovativeness. Few authors are able to draw together very different streams of literature, even fewer are able to ground their theory in extensive empirical research and, again, still fewer are able to come up with practical methods and frameworks.

Hence, more than a contribution to individual fields of research, Porter's main addition lies in the integration of various research approaches. Porter discusses the individual firm in relation to its industry and the macro-environment it operates in. The three schools discussed in the introduction of this chapter are therefore all present in *The Competitive Advantage of Nations*.

When a book written by an influential academic as Michael Porter appears, it is inevitable that the book is discussed and used widely. Since *The Competitive Advantage of Nations* appeared, the method described in it has been applied scores of times on countries, regions, industries, cities, clusters and even individual firms. The book has been reviewed and discussed extensively in academic journals (a good general discussion is Grant, 1991) and on conferences. It would be surprising if after having received so much attention, no extensions and criticism would have come up. It is only natural, and even quite positive for the creation of knowledge, that various authors have come up with new ideas inspired by Porter's work. Below some of the key points of critique have been summarized.

Limited attention for governmental policy. Several authors have criticized Porter for not paying enough attention to the role of government in the diamond framework. Most authors seem, however, to have misunderstood the role government can play in Porter's framework. The fact that it is seen as an influencing factor and not as a determinant does not mean that governmental policy has a negligible influence on the creation of national competitiveness. In fact, quite the contrary is the case and Porter's chapter on governmental policy is one of the largest in his book.

Van den Bosch and De Man (1994) have criticized Porter's view on government on three grounds. Firstly, they point to the fact that Porter has not incorporated local and regional governments in his discussion of government's role, but has limited himself to national government. As was shown in the section on the city level above, Porter has recently paid attention to this issue. Secondly, there is a shift in governmental policy from macro policy making towards policy directed at meso- and micro-levels (Branscomb, 1992; Ostry, 1990), which Porter does not account for. The more government will play a role on these lower levels, the more it will become intertwined with the diamond and the less clear it will be that government should be an influencing factor in the diamond and not a determinant. Thirdly, Porter does not relate the role of government to the industry life cycle. Porter does claim that in different stages of national competitive development, government plays a different role. Yet, the same effect can also be observed with regard to different phases of the industry life cycle. A government may be very active in the early phases of development, diminish in influence when the industry matures and may come back to play an important role in restructuring the industry in the decline phase. Incorporating these extensions in the Porter framework, would contribute to a more balanced understanding of the impact of government on competitiveness.

Limited attention for transnational business. Dunning (1992) adds transnational business activity (TBA) as an influencing factor to the diamond. He consistently works out the influence of TBA on every determinant. For example, a foreign multinational which locates itself in a country can be more demanding than the incumbent firms. Its demands can force suppliers to upgrade. Another possibility is that the firm makes the country aware of different consumer demands and thus stimulates the quality of demand in the home market. By incorporating transnational business activity as an influencing factor, Dunning has extended the diamond in keeping with Porter's ideas. It provides us with a tool which subscribes to Porter's views on inward and outward foreign direct investments, but which allows us to give a more detailed account of them.

Unclarity regarding the correct geographical level. The title of *The Competitive Advantage of Nations* suggests that it is a book which deals with the level of the nation state. Yet, many examples in the book concern the regional level while cross border clusters of firms can be distinguished as well. Rugman (1992) defends a so-called `double-diamond' approach to explain this. This approach suggests that firms in order to gain a competitive advantage should not just direct their strategies at their own diamond, but take markets in other countries into account as well. According to Rugman, a focus on clusters in the home country does not take into account the internationalization of competition. As Porter and Armstrong (1992) point out, this approach fails to distinguish between the geographic locus of competitive advantage and the geographic scope of competition. The place where the strategies are formed and sustained can be a small region, which can compete on a world wide basis. Firms can strengthen their international competitive position precisely by strengthening their home base.

A table developed by Jacobs and De Jong (1992) clarifies this and extends Porter's analysis of the correct geographical level (see table 6.3 for a recent version). They make a distinction between the geographic scale of the production network and the geographic scale of the market. They show that Porter's notion of clusters can include crossborder clusters and that the right geographical level of analysis is determined by the specific cluster. Some clusters can be regionally concentrated and compete in world markets (like for instance Dutch cut flowers), other clusters are characterized by international production networks and international markets. Table 6.3 gives some examples of relevant industries for the Netherlands. The strongest and most competitive clusters can be found in the lower left hand corner: regionally concentrated clusters competing on a world wide basis.

Extension of Porter's analysis of clusters. Jacobs and De Man (1996) extend the analysis of the cluster concept. As the cluster concept is not clearly defined by Porter, different ideas on what a cluster is, have come into being. The Dutch Ministry of Economic Affairs for example uses a much more limited definition of the cluster concept (see chapter 7). It defines clusters as networks of companies surrounding a core enterprise. Porter's conception of clustering is much broader. As the famous example of the cluster of the Italian ceramic tile industry shows, clusters can consist of equal companies as well. In order to get a firmer grip on the cluster concept Jacobs and De Man put forward several dimensions of clustering and relate them to feasible policies and strategies. In this way a menu of policies and strategies is created from which firms and governments can pick those elements which are most applicable to their specific needs. This method makes the idea of clusters as developed by Porter more tangible. The dimensions of clustering are the geographical scope of the cluster, the vertical, horizontal and lateral relations in it, the focal point(s) around which a cluster centers (e.g. a research institute, an entrepreneurial family), technological similarities and the quality of the network.

Table 6.3 Geographical scope of markets and production networks of selected industries in The Netherlands.

market / production	world	Europe	Netherlands
world	Telecommunications Recorded discs Long haul trade		
NW Europe		Trucks and lorries Plastics & polymers	
Netherlands	Machinery for the dairy industry Yacht building (top segment) Industrial textiles	Dairy industry Road transport	Engineering for the dairy industry Yacht building (lower segment)
regional	Cut flowers Greenhouse construction Cocoa Dredging	Copiers Short haul trade	Construction

Source: Jacobs and De Man (1996) based on strategic sector studies by TNO-STB.

Underestimating globalization. Ohmae (1990) claims that the lowering of trade barriers, the internationalization of capital markets etc. has made firms footloose. In his view, firms can establish themselves wherever they want. Globalization thus reduces the role of the place where a firm is established. Porter however argues, that the more international competition increases, the less firms are protected behind artificial barriers to competition and, consequently, the more they will have to draw on real capabilities and resources in order to be able to compete. These capabilities and resources lie to a large extent in the immediate environment of the firm, thus rendering the location of a firm more, not less, important. The internationalization of competition thus exposes the true strengths of countries. This counterintuitive finding appears to be consistent with research by Ruigrok and Van Tulder (1995), who find that the extent of globalization is often exaggerated.

Limited analysis of the role of culture

Even though Porter pays attention to the role of culture in creating competitive advantage, it remains unclear to what extent it is of relevance. Van den Bosch and Van Prooijen (1992) point to possibilities of extending Porter's analysis of culture, by using Hofstede's (1980) dimensions of national culture. They conclude that the attitude towards uncertainty and the masculine/feminine characteristics of a country can influence various aspects of the diamond. For example, if a country is characterized by avoidance of uncertainty, its firms may be more inclined to establish long-term relationships with their suppliers. Using Hofstede's dimensions may thus give a clearer insight into the impact of culture on country competitiveness.

Summary

Porter's *The Competitive Advantage of Nations* integrates various approaches to national competitiveness. His diamond framework and his ideas on clustering are grounded in a wealth of empirical and theoretical research. It has also proven to be applicable in practice and on different levels of analysis (the nation, the region, the city). Porter's explicit attempt to connect firm level processes to national processes holds important implications for managers and governments alike. Since the book appeared various extensions have been proposed, most of them within the context of Porter's original framework. The already remarkable richness of his analyses has only been extended since.

That his insights are relevant to practice as well, can be seen in the next two chapters. Two well-known Dutch policy makers discuss the way in which Porter has contributed to the formulation of policies in the Netherlands and the Port of Rotterdam.

References

Bosch, F.A.J. van den, and A.P. de Man, 1994, "Government's impact on the business environment and strategic management", *Journal of General Management*, Vol. 19, No. 3, pp. 50-59.

Bosch, F.A.J. van den, and A.A. van Prooijen, 1992, "The impact of national culture - a missing element in Porter's analysis?", *European Management Journal*, Vol. 10, No. 2, pp. 173-177.

Branscomb, L.M., 1992, "Does America need a technology policy?", *Harvard Business Review*, March/April, pp. 24-31.

Chandler, A.D., 1990, *Scale and Scope*, Cambridge (Mass.), The Belknap Press.

Dertouzos, M.L., R.K. Lester and R.M Solow, 1989, *Made in America*, Cambridge (Mass.), The MIT Press.

Dunning, J.H., 1992, "The competitive advantage of countries and the activities of transnational corporations", *Transnational Corporations*, Vol. 1, No. 1, pp. 135-168.

Ghemawat, P., 1991, *Commitment: The Dynamic of Strategy*, New York, The Free Press.

Grant, R.M., 1991, "Porter's Competitive Advantage of Nations: an Assessment", *Strategic Management Journal*, Vol. 12, pp. 535-548.

Hofstede, G., 1980, *Culture's Consequences*, Beverly Hills, Sage publications.

Jacobs, D., P. Boekholt and W. Zegveld, 1990, *De economische kracht van Nederland*, Den Haag, SMO.

Jacobs, D., and M.W. de Jong, 1992, "Industrial Clusters and the Competitiveness of the Netherlands: empirical and conceptual issues", *De Economist*, 140, No. 2, pp. 233-252.

Jacobs, D., and A.P. de Man, 1996, "Clusters, Industrial Policy and Firm Strategy: a Menu Approach", *Technology Analysis and Strategic Management*, Vol. 8, No. 4, forthcoming.

Krugman, P.R., "Competitiveness: A Dangerous Obsession", *Foreign Affairs*, March/April, pp. 28-44.

Metze, M., 1990, *Hoe flexibel is BV Nederland?*, Intermediair-rapport, Het Spectrum.

Nelson, R.R., 1991, "Why do firms differ, and how does it matter?", *Strategic Management Journal*, Vol. 12, pp. 61-74.

Ohmae, K., 1990, *The Borderless World*, London, Collins.

Ostry, S., 1990, "Government's & Corporations in a Shrinking World: trade & innovation policies in the United States, Europe & Japan", *Columbia Journal of World Business*, Spring/Summer, pp. 10-16.

Porter, M.E., 1992, "A note on Culture and Competitive Advantage: Response to Van den Bosch and Van Prooijen", *European Management Journal*, Vol. 10, No. 2, p. 178.

Porter, M.E., 1990, *The Competitive Advantage of Nations*, London, MacMillan.

Porter, M.E., 1995, "The Competitive Advantage of the Inner City", *Harvard Business Review*, May/June, pp. 55-71.

Porter, M.E., and W. Armstrong, 1992, "Canada at the Crossroads", *Business Quarterly*, Spring, pp. 6-10.

Rugman, A.M., 1992, "Porter takes the wrong turn", *Business Quarterly*, Vol. 56, No. 3, pp. 59-64.

Ruigrok, W., and R. van Tulder, 1995, *The Logic of International Restructuring*, London, Routledge.

7.

The Netherlands: more than flower power

L.A. Geelhoed (Secretary General of the Ministry of Economic Affairs of The Netherlands)

Introduction and relationship with The Netherlands

According to Michael Porter, The Netherlands is the country of cut flowers. He often uses the Dutch cut-flower sector to exemplify a competitive industry. Evidently, in Porter's vision our culture, passions and traditions make a good marriage with flowers. But fortunately, the Dutch economy encompasses more than tulips alone. Think for example of chemicals, transport and international services, each of which represents a cluster that is highly competitive by international standards. The application of Porter's methodology to the Netherlands has clearly pointed this out (Jacobs, Boekholt, Zegveld, 1990).

Nonetheless, the example of the Dutch cut-flower sector is in my view a delightful choice. Its exports are worth over one billion dollars a year which equals a share of 64% of the world market. In addition, the Dutch cut-flower sector is very modern. The products are characterized by innovation, upgrading, differentiation, quality, and freshness. The factors Michael Porter mentioned as responsible for this success are: the presence of research institutes, the Amsterdam airport Schiphol, a well-developed infrastructure, high quality domestic demand, healthy competition and the presence of competitive suppliers. The example is particularly delightful because it illustrates the importance of the

F.A.J. van den Bosch and A.P. de Man (eds.), Perspectives on Strategy, 61-66.
© 1997 *Kluwer Academic Publishers. Printed in the Netherlands.*

interplay of these factors so well. In short: it is the quintessential example of the diamond framework in action.

What is particularly appealing in Michael Porter's work is the bridge he strikes across the traditional gap between the macroeconomists/policy-makers on the one side and industry/strategic management on the other. This has made it easier for governments to implement effective policies. Equally appealing is the focus on firms as an integral part of their environment, and on the interrelationships between firms and research institutes. In addition, the knowledge infrastructure, sufficient competition and innovation are relevant issues for economic policy making, which are covered by Porter's work.

Competitiveness, the subject of *The Competitive Advantage of Nations*, is at the centre of attention as never before. One of the explanations for this unprecedented interest in the subject is the growing concern about loss of competitiveness and jobs in many places worldwide. This concern has of course also increased by the rapid emergence of new competitors (notably in South East Asia) as a part of the globalisation process.

Another cause of the growing interest in competitiveness is the disappointing economic development which we have been experiencing in Europe in recent years. The last cyclical trough painfully exposed the structural weaknesses of the European economy: unemployment rates are rising to record levels and the competitive position in high-tech sectors is rather weak. Precisely in such a period of downturn, pessimism is widespread, disadvantages stand out more clearly, and our own competitive advantages become harder to detect through the clouds of recession.

At such moments, the importance of clusters, which are normally only distinguishable by detailed research, comes clearly to the surface. Problems in a number of Dutch large enterprises reveal that they form the core of an extensive and widespread cluster: difficulties at the core are found to filter through fairly rapidly to peripheral areas of the cluster. Thereby illustrating the proposition that 'a cluster is as strong as its weakest link'. Therefore, strengthening clusters has become one of the main goals of Dutch economic policy. By stimulating the transfer of knowledge in clusters and forging links between business and research institutes, the government hopes to raise the innovativeness of the Dutch economy.

The Competitive Advantage of Nations was published at precisely the right moment for the Netherlands. The diamond sparkled in a policy document of the Dutch government, in which strengths and weaknesses of the Dutch economy were analysed (Ministry of Economic Affairs, 1990). The central question raised in the report is to what extent the Dutch economy is ready for the challenges of the 1990s. The report deals with this question with reference to three themes linked to the work of Michael Porter: the entrepreneurial climate, competition and cooperation in industry, and the necessity of constant innovation.

Most clearly, Porter's influence can be found in the cluster policy implemented by the Ministry. The Ministry has proposed and implemented various measures aimed at strengthening clustering (Ministry of Economic Affairs, 1995). The aim of cluster policy is defined as promoting strategic cooperation between technologically advanced companies and the public research infrastructure. Cluster projects can be funded by the government, provided that they match six criteria: the project must be a new strategic cooperation in R&D between a company and a Dutch research institute; internationally advanced technologies have to be developed or applied; the project must be sufficiently large; the project must have potential for the involvement of other companies; the involved research institute must have a strong knowledge base; the project must be economically and technically feasible.

Other cluster policies aim to stimulate the market orientation of research institutes and help SME's to find their way to specific technologies. Upgrading projects for suppliers and projects enhancing the cooperation between core firms and their main suppliers are supported as well.

Around 1990, not everybody was accustomed to this new view on knowledge, innovation and clustering. Today, however, it is safe to say that most Dutch policy-makers have grown used to the new approach. This revolution in economic thinking in the Netherlands is for a great part inspired by the work of Porter.

Some critical reflections

Besides all the appreciation for Porter's work there are still some critical reflections to be made. Although these reflections are more applicable to the users of Porter's work, than to Porter's work as such. From the perspective of the Dutch government three relevant critiques on Porter's work are of interest.

First of all, although the diamond thinking is very useful, it may not be allowed to persuade us to lose sight of macroeconomic conditions. A sound macroeconomic environment is not a universal panacea; it cannot make much but it can break a lot. Reliable macroeconomic fundamentals can be seen as a prerequisite for a favourable business climate. As a matter of fact, the World Bank only recently again demonstrated the importance of sound fundamentals (inflation, interest rate, budget deficits, etc.) as the starting-point for the development of the countries of South East Asia. Of course Porter does not claim that macroeconomic conditions are unimportant. But a strong diamond is not the only source of competitive advantage. It has to be embedded in a sound macroeconomic environment.

A second critique regards Porter's view of European unification. It is good for us Europeans for a person like Michael Porter to take a highly critical look at this. He postulates that the internal market has been created according to the obsolete concept of economies of scale, and that the internal market denies the need for more differentiation. Porter maintains that European integration will lead companies to compete on scale and cost, rather than enticing them to innovate and specialise in niches.

The internal market is a single large domestic market with 350 million critical consumers and free movement of goods, services, capital and persons. And because many previously sheltered markets are being opened up, competition in many sectors (also between governments) is growing. At the same time, defensive state subsidies to 'national champions' are no longer permitted. Certainly for the Netherlands, with the limited size of its home market and its traditionally international orientation, the internal market adds opportunities.

As a result of more flexible production processes, economies of scale may in the future take on a less important role, and advantages may be gained through differentiation. In my view, however, the internal market does not form a barrier to business strategies towards differentiation, exploration of niches and 'diseconomies of scale'. On the contrary, if we are able to create an internal market, open for international competition, this market will offer more and more attractive niches. Moreover, the internal market offers competitive firms a valuable springboard. In this respect I see the internal market as a stimulating condition, an incentive towards innovation and dynamism. A large and competitive internal market creates new opportunities for building a favourable home base and the importance of that favourable home base is just what Michael Porter once again demonstrated in his work.

The third and final difference between Porter's approach and that of a government official is the difference in perspective. Porter, as a professor of strategic management, regards the world through spectacles as worn by industry. Through these spectacles, everything is assessed as good if firms are able to produce more efficiently and less expensively. Government officials however, also have another perspective. And from that perspective, jobs and social stability are at least as important as returns and share prices. Major restructurings in the business world are therefore sometimes frowned upon by governments.

However, it would not be appropriate for policy-makers to point an accusing finger at all firms in the process of reorganizing their business and shedding personnel, since government and industry should be team-mates rather than opponents. When reorganizations are announced, many firms are already up to their knees in the mud, as it were, and if they fail to take suitable action they risk going under completely. With even more dramatic consequences for employment perspectives. In my view, the government therefore should adopt a discrete attitude. Competitiveness, and as a direct result prospects for employment, is determined within firms. For the government, the task that remains is primarily that of creating the proper conditions, a task which is becoming increasingly important under the pressure of growing global competition. Hence, I concur with Porter that government cannot create competitive advantages on its own, but that it has an important influencing role in the diamond.

Competitiveness and government policy
Porter has injected fresh life into the concept of competitiveness. According to conventional wisdom, countries have a comparative

advantage where production utilizes the abundant production factor. This view proved inadequate when it came to explaining competitiveness. For instance, it would be difficult to attribute the strong position of the Dutch horticulture industry to cheap labour or a favourable climate. Rather the innovations created by the horticulture firms have brought the Dutch cut flower industry the competitive strength it possesses.

Modern theory is more closely in tune with practice. Constant innovation and improvement of factor conditions yields competitive advantage. In this way countries are able to improve their competitiveness themselves, it is not manna from heaven. The government's role should not be considered in isolation, but more indirectly as that of a player influencing the diamond, creating the proper conditions. The role of government can be either protective or dynamizing (challenging, stimulating). I consider that this lesson has clearly penetrated into Dutch economic policy. Formerly, we had a lot of protective regulations and state aid with, retrospectively, comparatively little effectiveness (shipbuilding is a case in point, where state aid could not and did not prevent the demise of some Dutch producers). Economic policy nowadays aims for a more dynamic economy. This is not always easy to do, due to the opposition raised by imminent losers, while future winners are not yet present when deregulation measures are discussed.

One of Porter's main conclusions is that national prosperity is not inherited, but created. A nation's competitiveness depends on the capacity of its industry to innovate and upgrade. As I frequently notice, not everybody is aware of that. For future prosperity, that is a dangerous fact. The work of Michael Porter contributes to the awareness that prosperity is created. It is above all in emphasizing this, that Porter's work has made a valuable contribution to the policy debate in the Netherlands.

References

Jacobs, D., P. Boekholt, W. Zegveld, 1990, *De economische kracht van Nederland*, The Hague, SMO

Ministry of Economic Affairs, 1990, *Economie met open grenzen*, The Hague, Sdu

Ministry of Economic Affairs, 1995, *Kennis in beweging*, The Hague Sdu

8.

Rotterdam seen through Porter-coloured glasses

R.M. Smit (CEO Port of Rotterdam)

Introduction

The Municipality of Rotterdam is concerned with the creation and stimulation of a favourable atmosphere for economic activities. In this article a number of specific aspects of this regional economy are discussed based on the conceptual framework employed by Professor Porter. A clear qualification should be made here, however. Porter's book *The Competitive Advantage of Nations* (Porter, 1990) is primarily concerned with countries. When applying his method to a small region, a number of problems arise. Most relevant networks go beyond regional boundaries and have a national and sometimes international dimension.

Nevertheless, provided that it is sensibly applied, Porter's method can provide valuable insight into Rotterdam's economy. In Rotterdam, we find companies which benefit logistically from being located in the port region. Around these companies a cluster of businesses has come into being which greatly benefit from each other's vicinity.

Three clusters are dominant in the Rotterdam region:
I   The transport cluster
II   The petro-chemical cluster, and

F.A.J. van den Bosch and A.P. de Man (eds.), Perspectives on Strategy, 67-79.
© *1997 Kluwer Academic Publishers. Printed in the Netherlands.*

III   The food cluster.

First, I would like to discuss the transport cluster, then the chemical cluster and finally the food cluster. For each cluster I will summarize the main characteristics of the cluster, its (historical) development, the role of the Municipal Authority in it and, last but not least, the possibilities for future development.

The well known four determinants of Porter's diamond of competitive advantage will play a crucial role in our analyses: 1) factor conditions, 2) demand conditions, 3) related and supporting industries and 4) firm strategy, structure and rivalry. At the same time the role of the determinants in the different stages of Porter's development theory of competitive advantage will be used to analyse the (historical) development. Porter distinguishes four stages of competitive development: the factor driven stage, the investment driven stage, the innovation driven stage and the wealth driven stage.

The transport cluster
Main characteristics
Rotterdam accounts for approximately 45% of total transshipment in the Hamburg - Le Havre range. For containers this is 38%. Two-thirds of container transshipments - particularly industrial goods - is in transit to other European countries. Rotterdam is the European Mainport par excellence and the largest port in the world.

In 1990, 38,800 people worked in the Rotterdam region in sectors directly related to the maritime transport cluster: for example with stevedores, forwarding companies, ship brokers and transport companies. It accounts for some 10% of total employment in the Rotterdam region. This sector directly generates added value of more than 6 billion guilders: around 16% of the total added value in the region. This does not include the indirect effects emanating from suppliers and business services for example.

In spite of the impressive development of the transport cluster, the presence of companies which produce machines is limited practically to producers of cranes and tugboats and other specialized craft. If the Netherlands is taken as regional reference then the production of machines becomes more important (truck, trailers, etc.)

Development

It is self-evident that the presence of natural factors - the river Rhine and the vicinity of the sea for instance - played an important role in the initial phase of development of the transport cluster. The existence of specific Dutch skills, such as trading, was important as well. This stimulated the development of transport services which were closely interwoven with trade. In Porter terms this phase of development is called the factor driven phase.

At a second stage, created factors played a dominant role. Investment in the Euro-channel (Eurogeul), the excavation of harbours and the creation of port sites are a few examples. The existence of specific Dutch skills is also important here. Since 'water problems' are especially relevant in the Netherlands, knowledge was acquired to tackle vast hydraulic engineering projects in an efficient and innovative way. These are developments in what could be described as the hardware of the port (investment driven). They represent a competitive advantage. The courage and vision of the decision-makers at the time formed an essential element of the port's development.

In the next stage of Porter's theory, technological and organizational innovations are predominant. Where the Rotterdam region is concerned, examples of innovations are the construction of 'smart' transshipment terminals with modern transshipment technology, the presence of specialised suppliers such as crane manufacturers, the creation of networks of specialised logistic service companies and developments in inland shipping, such as push-towing and specialised scheduled container shipping.

The role of the Rotterdam Municipal Authority has constantly changed in this process. In joint consultation with trade and industry, the municipal authority developed and is still developing the required infrastructure. It has also performed a mediator role in shaping the labour system and labour conditions. Within Porter's framework, this is seen as improvement of the factor conditions. The Municipal Authority sometimes played an important role - via the Municipal Port Management - in generating an appropriate structure of industry. I am thinking here, for example, of the Port Management's stimulating role in relation to the setting up of ECT (European Container Terminus, the largest container terminal of the world). It allowed the company to quickly achieve a sufficient volume to develop the most advanced technology for container transshipment. At the same time the Municipality provided the conditions for the existence of internal competition in the container sector.

The Municipal Authority also plays either a stimulating or intermediary role in the creation of new business configurations which are better equipped to face the challenges of the future. A number of different restructuring processes have taken place in this way. Within Porter's framework, this can be seen as an intervention in the determinant firm strategy, structure and rivalry.

During the past few years, we have seen the role of the Municipal Authority shift towards stimulating the creation of networks, encouraging contacts and cooperation between different agents to generate innovative products. I will give some examples of this in the next section. I want to stress that of course the orientation towards innovation of the companies themselves - the firm strategy, in Porter terms - is what has been the decisive factor in the success of the Rotterdam transport cluster. The region has companies which have introduced highly innovative technologies. To quote a few examples: transshipment terminals where the most modern technology is used; the creation of push-tow inland shipping for bulk transport and the enormous development of container inland shipping thanks to investment in specialised vessels and organizational innovation.

Future perspectives

We are in the middle of a very impressive technological revolution, according to Giersch (1992) characterized by

- a greater role for knowledge creation, innovation and productivity advance as compared to the 1950s and the 1960s,
- a greater importance of entrepreneurship and intrapreneurship than in the decades of expansion,
- an increasing pervasiveness of competition in all forms: intra-firm, intraindustry, global, inter-locational, from above (product innovation), from below (process innovation), and from outside (potential competition of newcomers),
- a greater emphasis on flexibility -in contrast to size and scale economies (except for economies of scope in research and marketing),

- a greater concern for the human factor -in contrast to fixed capital- and for general education, professional education, job rotation, quality circles, team spirit, and team leadership
- lean production with world-wide sourcing,
- a decentralization of decision making (along the lines of the subsidiarity principle), and even,
- a decentralization of production,
- the transformation of big business into conglomerates of independent business units.

This technological revolution will have far-reaching consequences for logistic systems, of which the port forms a part. The growing significance of knowledge and information, the consequences of the process of globalisation, the increasing integration of technology, production and logistics and the customization trend, are only some of the challenges to the logistic system of Rotterdam.

In addition, Europeanization will probably bring about a shift in the boundaries of what is seen as the Rotterdam cluster today. This makes a stronger embedding in a European logistic network essential. In order to achieve this, new innovative developments are necessary in infrastructure, information flows, knowledge of the subject matter and the nature of the services provided.

Overseas exporters of industrial goods are centralising their stocks in fewer distribution centres with a wider radius. In this way specialised European distribution is created. The Netherlands is taking advantage of this last trend. Forty percent of the American and Japanese companies which have chosen to have a European Distribution Centre have opted for the Netherlands. In the past years, three-quarters of the new European Distribution Centres have been set up in the Netherlands. The resulting employment is estimated at around 20,000 jobs. Indirect employment is estimated at a total of some 30,000 jobs. The strength of the mainports Rotterdam and Schiphol and their related logistic networks are an important factor in their choice of the Netherlands by these companies.

Together with industry, Rotterdam's Municipal Authority wishes to take maximal advantage of the developments I have outlined by means of various initiatives. These initiatives can be related to the determinants of Porter's diamond.

Factor improvement

- Development of infrastructure such as new container terminals at the 'Maasvlakte' (an area relatively recently reclaimed from the sea), and facilities for railways, barge and truck transportation in the port area.
- Advocation of the construction of new connections with the hinterland, such as the so-called 'Betuwelijn', a railway connection for goods transportation connecting Rotterdam and the Netherlands with Germany and East-Europe.

Firm Strategy, Structure and Rivalry

- Stimulation of the flexibilization of labour in the port region, in deliberation with trade-unions and employer organizations.
- Advocation of the liberalisation of railway transportation in the Netherlands and Europe, to break with the monopoly structure in this sector, allowing the operation of new firms with new innovative products.

Forming of Networks

- The development of Distriparks with a European dimension. In Distriparks storage and distribution activities of industrial goods are clustered in the vicinity of container terminals. This results in important synergetic effects, bringing the quality of the logistic services to a higher level.
- Stimulating (together with firms) the construction of optimal links with industrial centres and goods distribution centres in the hinterland. An example of this is the development of new services like shuttle services (trains connecting other European cities directly to Rotterdam) and telematics facilities.
- The development of information technology applications in order to raise information flows between the different parties to a higher level of quality. This creates conditions to allow the parties in the logistic chain to introduce new logistic products and optimise logistic processes. INTIS (International Transport Information System) was set up together with PTT-Telecom and trade and industry. This organization develops different applications for the use of information technology in the port cluster.
- Rotterdam Internal Logistics. In order to improve the quality of international logistic processes in the port, the Port Management and the business community set up the

Rotterdam Internal Logistics Foundation. This organization is concerned, for example, with projects such as the development of a 4-TEU truck (a truck able to transport 4 twenty foot long containers), the floating container terminal, night-driving and the introduction of a 'smart card' for transport companies calling at the container terminals.

- A final example of network formation is a combined study by the municipal authority and the business community, aimed at creating a framework for logistic service companies 'to do more with the cargo'. We are taking a look at potential new activities of logistic service companies which thereby generate extra added value in the value chain.

The final comment I wish to make regarding the transport cluster concerns the fact that the Municipal Authority wishes to use Rotterdam's position as a Mainport to expand our profile as a European city. We want to raise the level of business services and the trade function of the region, as well as research and developments activities. For these activities, the improvement of the social infrastructure and the quality of life of the urban agglomeration is of crucial importance. The construction of the high quality office complex at 'Kop van Zuid' will make an important contribution towards achieving this.

The (petro)chemical cluster
Main characteristics
In the Rotterdam region the (petro)chemical cluster is a very crucial factor. The Rotterdam petrochemical complex generates 35% of the direct added value of the port complex. If supply activities are also taken into account this share increases to about 50%. In the oil and chemical sectors almost 14,000 people were employed in 1990, of which 8,500 in the chemical industries and 5,300 in oil refineries. The added value of these activities was about 4 billion guilders. In these figures indirect effects, which for the chemical sector are very important, are not included. The share of the added value of the Rotterdam's chemical sector in the total value added of that industry in the Netherlands was about of 20% in 1988. For the refineries this was about 90%. This is much more than the share of the Rotterdam region in the GDP of the Netherlands, which is about 10%.

Development

Seen in a historical perspective the accessibility of Rotterdam for huge vessels played an important role in the development of this cluster, because being located in Rotterdam implied an important logistic advantage for the refineries, especially for the so-called balancing refineries. These are flexible refineries that can produce a mix of differentiated products with various specifications, suitable to meet every market demand. The crude oil used in the production process is coming by sea and a part of the produced oil products are also transported by sea-going vessels.

The proximity of refineries attracted many basic-chemical industries to the Rotterdam region, because oil products constitute the most important input for these industries. Other agglomeration advantages also played an important role. For example, oil and chemical companies have to meet more or less the same security and environmental requirements and can take advantage of the same pool of specialized labour in the region (process operators, chemical technicians, etc.).

At a later stage Rotterdam attracted chemical companies, which are not directly related to refineries, but to the basic-chemical industry. Around these chemical companies a network of suppliers of goods and services has arisen, like pipe-fitting companies, cleaning services, repairing services, suppliers of pipelines, suppliers of metal tanks, specialized logistic services, etc. Moreover many trading companies specialized in chemical products are located in Rotterdam, because in spite of the progress in communication technology, a location in the vicinity of production and storage of chemical products still provides an important advantage.

Despite its enormous volume, the Rotterdam petrochemical cluster is in some sense unilaterally developed. A large part of the production concerns bulk chemical products, although the so called specialties (tailor made specialized intermediate products) are not unimportant en probably will become even more important. The production of fine chemicals (end products) is limited. The Rotterdam companies are mostly production units of multinational chemical concerns. The head-quarters of these concerns, with the exception of Shell, are not established in Rotterdam. This is also the case for laboratories and other research and development activities. This unilateral character of the (petro)chemical cluster makes it vulnerable for possible future developments. However, the fact that in Rotterdam a wide spectrum of products is available is a favourable condition for a further development of the chemical cluster. Historically speaking, the role of the Municipal Authority in the petrochemical cluster was to develop the infrastructure in cooperation with the private sector and other governmental organisations: land, harbours basins, pipeline streets, roads, canals, railways, etc.

Future perspectives
According to different experts (Centraal Planbureau, 1992) a large part of the growth of the chemical industry in West-Europe will take place in the so-called specialties and the fine-chemicals products, while a relative stagnation of the bulk-chemistry, so dominant in Rotterdam, is expected. This means that Rotterdam, building upon its present strong position, has to attract more activities of the growing niches of the market, enhancing the variety of the chemical cluster. Because the logistic process will become even more important in the chemical industry and logistics become a more distinguishing factor in the competition in this industry, enhancing the link of the transport cluster with the chemical cluster becomes a major strategic objective. Particularly the position of Rotterdam as the most important container complex of West-Europe provides possibilities in this sense. Forging this link should strengthen the position of both clusters and could lead to new creative tailor made solutions for clients, while taking maximal advantage of the regional possibilities.

The policies of the Municipality in this sector are the following:

Factor Improvement
- to keep its traditional role in constructing and maintaining the necessary infrastructure such as the availability of land and the accessibility to the hinterland
- to look, together with the industry, for the availability and development of the labour force, in quantitative as well as in qualitative terms
- to enhance the location conditions for the industry by identifying and removing bottlenecks together with the business community.

Firm strategy, structure and rivalry
- to improve the marketing of the region; orienting it to the growing segments of the market and attracting companies that are introducing innovative technologies.

Forming of Networks
- to intensify, together with the business community, the links between the chemical and the transport cluster.

The food cluster
Main characteristics
In 1990, the food product industry in the Rotterdam region provided direct employment for approximately 7,700 people. This field of industry also directly generated added value totalling 800 million guilders. This sector is not only strong in the Rotterdam region, but also in other regions of the Netherlands. This makes this industry's share in regional employment more or less equal to that in the Netherlands.

Companies which achieve logistic advantages by locating close to deep water are strongly represented in the Rotterdam region. The raw materials used by these companies largely come by water. Part of their finished products can also be transported by water. Examples include the grain and oilseed processing industries, flour and margarine manufacturers and coffee-roasting houses. Above that, there are many industries which supply elements for the food industry, such as weighing-machines, box-makers, crates and pallets and bottle-machines.

Rotterdam also plays a leading role in the distribution of fruit, fruit juices and meat. This role is not limited to the Netherlands, but also applies to Europe. Where trade is concerned, the wholesale business in fruit and vegetables plays an important role, as well as that in fish, shellfish and mollusc, food and drink and machines for the food product industry. The laboratory for the most important Dutch food product companies, Unilever, is located in the region as well. It can therefore be concluded that the food cluster is reasonably well-developed, both in breadth (number of industries) and in depth (all phases of production are present).

Development
In the development of this cluster, like in the other clusters, originally natural factors played an important role: the logistic advantage of Rotterdam's location. The role of the Municipal Authority in this cluster is principally aimed at developing the infrastructure, the factor-determinant. Secondly at stimulating the formation of networks. This approach has encouraged new innovative combinations.

An illustration of this is the development of distribution activities in the field of fruit and fruit juices in the so-called Fruitport. The important fruit element in Dutch eating habits - a demand factor in Porter's diamond - and the logistic facilities in Rotterdam (a factor condition in Porter's diamond) form the basis of developments in the distribution of fruit and fruit juices. It contributed to the development of importers with very specialised knowledge and specialised logistic service companies which can comply with the specific demands of the sector: an advanced factor condition. Their influence extends beyond the Netherlands. Rotterdam is a distribution centre for fruit and fruit juices with a very important European dimension.

Due to a lack of innovation and failure to invest in time in specialised transshipment installations, Rotterdam received a major setback in the early eighties (this was probably an element of the wealth driven stage of development). Banana transshipment went to Antwerp which had an automated installation to unload boxes of bananas. A particularly remarkable fact is that this unloading installation was designed by a Dutch supplier who formed part of the Rotterdam cluster. Due to lack of interest in Rotterdam, he took his innovative design to Antwerp.

Future developments
In order to cope with the demands of the future, the Food Port concept needs to be further developed. The Rotterdam Fruitport project translates this into concrete terms. The Vierhavens-Merwehaven area is being developed into a European logistic centre for vegetables, fruit and fruit juices, including the processing industry along with supplying and supporting activities. Furthermore, linking the logistic system for the import of fruit and fruit juices with the 'Westland'[1]

---

[1] The Westland is a strong cluster of organizations centered around the production of vegetables and flowers in greenhouses, situated between Rotterdam and The Hague.

system for production, distribution and export of vegetables could make the Rotterdam/Westland region a large-scale logistic centre. This could make Rotterdam the front-door for European wholesale organizations.

The realization of an Agricultural Distribution Centre could mean a major step forward in this respect. The distribution activities of Westland could be clustered in such a centre. Furthermore, the link with the import flows of vegetables, fruit and fruit juices could take place there, bringing the quality of the logistic services to a higher level. We, as Rotterdam's Municipal Authority, play an initiating role and provide incentives in this process, encouraging the formation of networks.

Concluding remarks

This was a brief summary of the conceptual framework of Porter applied to developments in the Rotterdam region. The development of the different clusters in breadth (number of industries) and depth (phases of production) can be summarized as in table 8.1.

The role of the Municipal Authority has evolved through time. In addition to the classic role of supplier of infrastructure with some interventions in firm strategy, structure and rivalry, new tasks have emerged with an emphasis on the development of innovative networks.

Table 8.1: Clusters in the Port of Rotterdam

	Rotterdam		The Netherlands	
	Depth	Breadth	Depth	Breadth
Transport	-	++	+	++
Food	+	++	++	+++
(Petro)chemical	-	++	-	+++

Source: INRO/TNO, 1990 -: low +: moderate ++: high +++: very high

The wealth driven phase of competitive development is a phase we want to keep at a distance as far as possible. The loss of the banana trade, that I just mentioned, in the early eighties is a good example that we must not forget. Although I firmly believe that we have to cooperate in a number of fields, competition with neighbouring ports has its good aspects in this respect. It stimulates and motivates us and ultimately leads to innovations and a better product.

References

Centraal Planbureau, 1992, *Nederland in Drievoud*, The Hague, The Netherlands.

Giersch, Herbert, 1992, "Technology, Internationalization and Market Structures", in: *Proceedings of the International Conference "Scanning the Future; perspectives for the World Economy up to 2015"*, Centraal Planbureau, The Hague, The Netherlands.

INRO-TNO, 1990, *Rijnmond Kennisregio Rapportage Eerste Fase, Identificatie van Competitieve Subsectoren in Rijnmond*, Delft.

Porter, M.E., 1990, *The Competitive Advantage of Nations*, New York, Free Press.

9.

From positions to places?

Ard-Pieter de Man

Introduction

Michael Porter's three most influential books, *Competitive Strategy* (1980), *Competitive Advantage* (1985) and *The Competitive Advantage of Nations* (1990) have been subject to much discussion in both academics and business, as the previous chapters in this book have shown. Different adaptations, extensions and critiques of his various theories have been put forth. But how do his different books connect? Do they form a coherent body of knowledge or can changes in Porter's view on competitive advantage be discerned?

Research has looked into the development of Porter's thinking from different perspectives. His work has among others been analyzed from the perspective of his research method (Foss, 1996) and has been criticized by postmodern philosophers (Knights, 1992). Undoubtedly, someone will shortly publish a paper about a feminist perspective on Porter, the Freudian interpretation of his theories or Porter's role in the class struggle. The road taken to evaluate Porter's work in this chapter will be less colourful, but hopefully of more use to business. The point of departure will be Porter's view on competition (also see De Man, 1994). Competition can come in many forms and the way one perceives competition in an industry will determine the strategy chosen by a

F.A.J. van den Bosch and A.P. de Man (eds.), Perspectives on Strategy, 81-90.
© 1997 *Kluwer Academic Publishers. Printed in the Netherlands.*

firm. The increasing relevance of innovation will, for example, require a different attitude from firms than before.

Below, the strategy guidelines Porter suggests in *Competitive Strategy* will be compared with those in *The Competitive Advantage of Nations*. As an entire decade separates these books, it is hardly surprising that these guidelines diverge: in 1980 for example, demanding clients are seen as a threat to profitability, whereas in 1990 Porter believes that they stimulate innovativeness and thus strengthen competitive advantage. Whether this means that Porter is inconsistent or has changed his view on strategy and competition, remains however to be seen. Rather, it seems plausible that Porter deals with different kinds of competition in these two books. In competition theory these two kinds of competition are known as static and dynamic competition. It will be argued that Porter's first book is mainly relevant in situations of static competition, while a firm facing dynamic competition requires strategies along the lines laid out in his 1990 book on national competitiveness.

Static versus dynamic competition

For analyzing Porter's work, it suffices here to distinguish two kinds of competition: static and dynamic. Some of their key characteristics have been defined in table 9.1.

Table 9.1: Differences between static and dynamic competition

Static competition	Dynamic competition
• Focus on cost	• Focus on innovation
• Established firms compete	• New entrepreneurs
• Marginal improvements in existing products and processes, within existing market structures	• Continuous renewal of products, processes and market structures
• Exploitation of economies of scale and scope key to competitive advantage	• Learning and flexibility are the key to competitive advantage

Static competition refers to the kind of competition in which established firms, with existing products and production processes vie for market share and profits. In the case of static competition firms can only create and sustain a competitive advantage when they specialize on certain niches (differentiation, focus) or when they are better than other firms in driving down costs. Consequently, the exploitation of economies of scale and scope is essential in this kind of competition. As improvements in products and processes are limited, no new markets are created. In static competition, rivalry takes place in a given market structure (Knudsen, 1995).

Dynamic competition is present in an industry when firms compete with innovations and when new entrepreneurial firms come into being. This kind of competition has been analysed in theory by people like Schumpeter (1949). In the case of dynamic competition firms can only gain a competitive advantage when they surpass other firms in building competences which allow the firm to come up with new products and processes ahead of its competitors. New market structures are continuously created and former structures destroyed. In order to be able to renew its products and processes continuously, the firm must be able to learn new things quickly and to develop knowledge itself. Flexibility and entrepreneurship are the key words in dynamic competition.

Some industries are mainly characterized by static competition, others mostly by dynamic competition. In principle, all industries can be renewed after prolonged periods of static competition (Baden-Fuller and Stopford, 1992). An example is the steel industry, where the laws of competition dictated that economies of scale were crucial to competitive advantage until mini-mills were able to serve a differentiated set of customers and put the industry on its head. In other cases it may be possible that dynamic industries stabilize into a situation of static competition. This does not mean that the industry has become boring and sleepy. Static competition does not exclude fierce rivalry: cutthroat competition on cost is an example of this. The difference between static and dynamic competition implies no value judgement. It merely points out that there are different ways of competing, each requiring a different strategic attitude from firms.

Static and dynamic competition may alternate over the lifecycle of an industry. Currently, it is widely believed that dynamic competition is becoming more important in all industries and that this tendency is here to stay (see for example D'Aveni, 1994). It is possible that static and dynamic competition take turns in individual industries, so that periods of innovative disruption of the laws of competition are replaced by periods of relative stability in the sense that competition takes place with existing products in existing markets. More likely is that there is no dichotomy between static and dynamic competition, but that in the same industry firms can be found which focus on static competition and others which aim to innovate. In this view, competition takes place along a continuum between the two extremes of static and dynamic competition.

Whatever view one chooses, one's thinking about the fundamentals of competition is of great relevance for the strategy guidelines one prescribes to companies. Michael Porter's work is a good example of this. Below the idea will be advanced that Porter provides different strategy guidelines in 1980 and 1990, and that this can be explained by the fact that Porter has shifted from a perspective of static competition in 1980 to one of dynamic competition in 1990.

Strategy guidelines in 1980 and 1990

Table 9.2 presents an overview of some of the guidelines implicit in *Competitive Strategy* and *The Competitive Advantage of Nations*. Three aspects have been chosen to describe these guidelines: Porter's view on competitors, consumers and suppliers. These three were chosen on the ground that Porter discusses all three of them in both books.

Table 9.2: Porter's view on competitors, clients and suppliers

	1980	1990
Competitors	• Lessen the firm's profits and hence must be avoided	• Stimulate a firm to look for new products, markets etc. and hence should be confronted
Consumers	• Make expensive demands and bargain for lower prices	• Force a company to innovate and show future develop-ments
Suppliers	• Try to appropriate a firm's profits a.o. by raising their prices	• Can be a source of new ideas and can co-develop innovations

Source: De Man, 1995

Essentially in 1980 Porter sees competitors, consumers and suppliers as a threat to the return on investment of a firm, because all three of them will try to advance their position at the expense of the focal firm. In 1990 on the contrary, they are seen as beneficial to the firm because the most demanding competitors, consumers and suppliers force the company to stay awake, so to speak, and to look for improvements continuously. Porter himself has acknowledged the differences between his books, when he wrote about his policy prescriptions in 1990: "These prescriptions seem counterintuitive. The ideal would seem to be the stability growing out of obedient customers, captive and dependent suppliers, and sleepy competitors. Such a search for a quiet life, an understandable instinct, has led many companies to buy direct competitors or form alliances with them. In a closed, static world, monopoly would indeed be the most comfortable and profitable solution for companies. In reality, however competition is dynamic. Firms will lose to other firms who come from a more dynamic environment" (pp. 586/587).

In *Competitive Strategy* competitors are seen as a threat to profitability, but in Porter's later work he recognizes that the presence of competitors can also be stimulating. They can point in the direction of new products, production processes or markets. When a company is confronted with strong competition it is forced to upgrade and renew itself constantly. In the absence of such rivalry the firm may be lulled to sleep. Consequently, in the long run competition is advantageous.

Likewise, consumers can be seen as a nuisance in that they can be demanding and constantly pressure for lower prices. On the other hand, demanding consumers represent an opportunity as well. Like competitors they can force a company to innovate. More important, they can aid the company in defining new wishes for products and services. When a company is able to attract a set of demanding clients it may be able to come up with new products ahead of its competitors.

Finally, suppliers are mainly seen as a threat to profitability in the 1980 book. In 1990 however, Porter found that suppliers can be an important source of innovative ideas which can underpin a firm's competitive position. The positive effect of networks in stimulating technological innovations has been widely established in research in the course of the 1980s. Suppliers can help a firm in developing products or come up with ideas about smoothing the production process. In some industries firms rely to a large extent on the knowledge and capabilities of their networks (Lorenzoni and Baden-Fuller, 1995).

From positions...

In *Competitive Strategy* the emphasis lies on the position a firm should pick in an industry in order to remain profitable. This position should be either a low cost, differentiated or focus position (see chapters 2 and 3 in this book). Mintzberg (1990) sees Porter's *Competitive Strategy* as one of the most important books in the tradition of what he calls the positioning school. In this school, strategies are seen as positions in the market place. The market structure (in terms of the five forces identified by Porter), determines to a large extent which generic strategy is to be followed.

Strategizing in this way of thinking requires a thorough analysis of the market structure, which will lead a firm to pick a certain strategic position in that industry. Hence, it is a rather rational and clear approach to formulating strategy.

One of the critiques on Porter's approach in *Competitive Strategy* is that sometimes low cost and differentiation can be realized simultaneously. The classic example is that Japanese car manufacturers through the implementation of the innovation of the just-in-time system, have been able to lower their cost while simultaneously increasing the number of product varieties (differentiation).

The counterargument to this example is that in 1980 Porter abstracted from the phenomenon of innovation. In markets in which innovation is not of much importance or in which the time span between different innovations is considerable, the three generic strategies are still a very useful guideline to healthy strategizing.

The application of Porter's ideas from *Competitive Strategy* is restricted to the situation of static competition; that is the situation in which innovation does not constantly open up competition. As no industry is constant in a state of turbulence, the three generic strategies may be applicable in many situations and guide firms to decide on the position they aim for in the industry.

...to places?

Whereas *Competitive Strategy* dealt with the case of static competition, *The Competitive Advantage of Nations* discusses strategy in the case of dynamic competition. Dynamic competition is characterized by the continuous ebb and flow of innovations, whether product, process, organizational or any other kind of innovation. In the case of dynamic competition, a firm's task is to renew constantly and to keep up with the rapid pace of competition.

This task is simplified when a firm is located in a business environment which stimulates, challenges or even forces the firm to change. Instead of the position in the product market, the more interesting thing for a firm in a dynamic context is the choice of the place where it locates itself. Porter found that the location of the firm to a large extent determines its competitive advantage. Maintaining close contact with demanding customers, high quality suppliers, strong competitors and a well-developed pool of production factors stimulates the innovativeness of firms.

In a world so widely believed to be globalizing, the conclusion that place matters so much appears to be a paradoxical one. Yet, under closer scrutiny it appears to be logical. Practically any competitive advantage can be imitated in a globalizing economy, except for the ones which are rooted in highly local conditions. Behind the market position of a firm, lies a system of resources and capabilities which enables firms to come up with new products and services again and again. Porter found that this system is not only internal to the firm, but that it also comprises a set of interacting determinants in the firm's business environment (see chapters 6, 7 and 8). Simply put: the business environment a firm encounters, influences its production process and can stimulate a firm to innovate.

This view of the firm as being innovative and developing new competences is related to another of Mintzberg's schools of thought in strategy: the learning school. What Porter in effect says in *The Competitive Advantage of Nations* is that firms can learn from their competitors, buyers and suppliers, and use the acquired knowledge to innovate. Strategizing in this way of thinking is emergent and not completely controllable by the firm. It is quite different from the clearcut approach put forth in *Competitive Strategy*. When competition is dynamic it is impossible to have a clear, causal way of strategizing.

The turbulence and uncertainty of dynamic competition require a flexible learning approach instead.

Can these two be reconciled?
As stated before, the two approaches found in *Competitive Strategy* and *The Competitive Advantage of Nations* are applicable in different situations. The approach of *Competitive Strategy* is applicable when competition is static. The fact that innovation is hardly mentioned in the book is an indication of this. In contrast, *The Competitive Advantage of Nations* has the phenomenon of innovation as its central point of concern: constant renewal of products and processes are considered to be the core of competitive advantage.

Figure 9.1: From resources to market

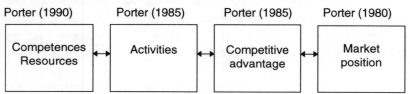

Figure 9.1 presents the relation between static and dynamic competition in another way. The figure shows that a firm combines its competences and resources in certain activities in the value chain (Porter, 1985). If it does so in a smart way it can create a competitive advantage which can underpin a certain position in the market (a low cost, differentiated or focus position). When competition is static, changes in product market positions are slow and incremental. This means that a strategy can be aimed at underpinning that position along the lines laid out by Porter in 1980, without running the risk that the position will come under severe pressure.

When, however, competition is dynamic market positions are only tenable for a short period of time, because new innovative products succeed each other at a rapid pace. This means that firms should not focus too much on maintaining a certain market position, but are better advised to develop the capabilities to renew their market positions. In terms of figure 9.1 this means that they have to develop their competences and must be able to upgrade their resources. Porter's *The*

Competitive Advantage of Nations gives some important guidelines for how this can be done (see table 9.2).

Concluding, in static competition market positions are important and *Competitive Strategy* presents good guidelines. In dynamic competition on the other hand, competences are relevant and *The Competitive Advantage of Nations* is a useful book. Dynamic competition pushes management to look upstream in the chain of causality depicted in figure 9.1. In this figure, the 1985 book *Competitive Advantage* can be found back in the relation between activities and competitive advantage.

Summary

In Porter's work different conceptions of competition can be found: static and dynamic competition. For each of these Porter has developed different policy guidelines. This does not mean that Porter's work is inconsistent: rather it means that the strategy to follow depends on the situation a firm encounters in its industry. Each strategy has to be shaped according to the specific environment a firm encounters. A general guideline is that when competition is static Porter's 1980 book is useful, while his 1990 book applies to situations in which competition is dynamic.
Porter's ability to think in different ways of competition and develop policy guidelines in accordance with these, is a rare talent. His ability to renew, makes him one of the most interesting strategy researchers of this time.

References

Baden-Fuller, C., and J.M. Stopford, 1992, *Rejuvenating the Mature Business*, London, Routledge.

D'Aveni, R.A., 1994, *Hypercompetition*, New York, The Free Press.

De Man, A.P., 1994, "1980, 1985, 1990: A Porter Exegesis", *Scandinavian Journal of Management*, Vol. 10, No. 4, pp. 437-450.

De Man, A.P., 1995, "Over kosten, kennis en clusters", in: Jacobs, D. and A.P. de Man (eds.), *Clusters en Concurrentiekracht*, Alphen aan den Rijn, Samsom BedrijfsInformatie, pp. 11-23.

Foss, N.J., 1996, "Research in strategy, economics, and Michael Porter", *Journal of Management Studies*, Vol. 33, No. 1, pp. 1-24.

Knights, D., 1992, "Changing Spaces: the disruptive impact of a new epistemological location for the study of management", *Academy of Management Review*, No. 3, pp. 514-536.

Knudsen, C., 1995, "Theories of the firm, strategic management, and leadership", in: C.A. Montgomery (ed.), *Resource-Based and Evolutionary Theories of the Firm: Towards a Synthesis*, Boston, Kluwer Academic Publishers, pp. 179-217.

Lorenzoni, G., and C. Baden-Fuller, 1995, "Creating a Strategic Center to Manage a Web of Partners", *California Management Review*, Vol. 37, No. 3., pp. 146-163.

Mintzberg, H., 1990, "Strategy Formation: Schools of Thought", in: Frederickson, J.W. (ed.), *Perspectives on Strategic Management*, New York, Harper Business, pp. 105-235.

Porter, M.E., 1980, *Competitive Strategy*, New York, The Free Press.

Porter, M.E., 1985, *Competitive Advantage*, New York, The Free Press.

Porter, M.E., 1990, *The Competitive Advantage of Nations*, London, MacMillan Press.

Schumpeter, J.A., 1949, *The Theory of Economic Development*, Cambridge Mass., Harvard University Press.

10.

Porter's contribution to more general and dynamic strategy frameworks

Frans A.J. van den Bosch

Introduction

Understanding why firms are successful is a very basic question in strategy both from a practitioner and a research perspective. In the strategy and management literature, however, we are confronted with different analytical frameworks, applicable at different levels of analysis such as the industry and the national level, providing different answers! Needless to say there is a clear necessity to create more integrative strategy frameworks. This concluding chapter is devoted to this topic by briefly describing Porter's contribution to a more integrated and dynamic strategy framework.

Table 10.1 presents basic questions and problems strategy research is currently facing. The basic questions in strategy all deal with the search for determinants of firm success. Although over time different analytical frameworks have been developed, a basic problem in strategy research is how to integrate these frameworks. This gives rise to a basic challenge in strategy research especially if such more integrative frameworks are of a dynamic nature. Dynamic frameworks provide us with answers that go beyond understanding why firms are

F.A.J. van den Bosch and A.P. de Man (eds.), Perspectives on Strategy, 91-100.
© *1997 Kluwer Academic Publishers. Printed in the Netherlands.*

successful at a given point in time. The real challenge is to understand why firms are successful over time. That is to understand *the dynamic processes* by which firms create and attain superior and sustainable competitive positions. In my opinion, Porter has made a major contribution to this subject in his article "Towards a dynamic theory of strategy", published in a special issue of the Strategic Management Journal (Winter 1991) devoted to the topic of "Fundamental Research Issues in Strategy and Economics".

Table 10.1: Basic questions and problems in strategy

Basic questions in strategy:
Why are firms successful? Why do firms attain superior and sustainable competitive positions? What are the determinants of firm success over time? Are some determinants more basic than others?

Basic problem in strategy research:
Different analytical frameworks with different perspectives on the role of time in strategy at different levels of strategy provide different answers.

Challenge for strategy research:
Can these different frameworks be integrated into more general and dynamic frameworks and if so, how?

Example:
How to connect Porter's Five Forces Framework (industry level), Value Chain Framework (business level) and Diamond Framework (national level)?

Source: Author

The purpose of this chapter is to give a brief sketch of Porter's dynamic theory of strategy and by doing so to integrate the different frameworks discussed in the previous chapters into a more general and dynamic strategy framework.

Towards the origins of competitive advantage
The basic question in strategy "Why are firms successful?" can in principle be answered in two distinct ways: a static and a dynamic way. The static approach deals with the question "Why are firms successful at a given point *in* time?", that is given a particular

competitive position of the firm. The dynamic approach deals with the dynamic process by which firms create and attain competitive positions. This approach focuses on the dynamic version of the basic question in strategy, that is "Why are firms successful *over* time?". Table 10.2 summarizes the key questions and issues of the static and dynamic approach. The questions raised in table 10.2 illustrate that the dynamic approach highlights the process dimension of strategy as discussed in chapter 1.

Table 10. 2:Basic questions in the static and dynamic approach to strategy

STATIC APPROACH   *Why are firms successful at a given point in time?*   a) What are the causes of superior firm performance at a given point in time?   b) What makes some industries and some positions within industries more attractive than others?   **DYNAMIC APPROACH**   *Why are firms successful over time?*   a) By which processes do firms attain a superior position?   b) Why is a particular firm able to get into an advantaged position?

Source: Author, based on Porter (1991)

The importance of distinguishing a static and dynamic approach in strategy becomes clear when one is interested in the origins of competitive advantage of firms. For example, it is tempting to analyze a firm's success in terms of the attractiveness of the industry structure and of the positioning of that particular firm within this industry. Although such an analysis is fruitful, it delves not deep enough to be helpful for practitioners, because we want to understand why a firm has an attractive position within the industry. This understanding can be of help for protecting and improving such a position. However, having analyzed why a firm has an attractive position within an industry in terms of cost, differentiation and scope of activities, the next question arises: "Why does that happen?" This means that we can keep delving towards a series of mutual related basic questions, labeled by Porter as the chain of causality.

Chain of causality

Porter's concept of the chain of causality visualizes the search for the origins of success of firms. The chain consists of a number of successive links. Each link deals with a question and a (partial) answer to that question. For our purpose it is interesting to note that each link represents more or less one of Porter's frameworks such as his Five Forces framework and Value chain framework. Porter describes his chain of causality as representing "the determinants of success in distinct businesses". Looking in that way to the chain of causality shows in a sense the "determinants of determinants" of firm success over time as illustrated by figure 10.1. This figure is based on Porter's graphical illustration of the chain of causality. I added to his figure the notion of links, numbered one to five and supplemented the figure with the diamond framework as the last and sixth link, in figure 10.1. The dotted line indicates the "barrier" between the static and dynamic approach. The first approach is labeled by Porter as the cross-sectional problem in strategy in which, as is pointed out above, a given competitive position has to be explained. Below this barrier, indeed a barrier in theories of strategy, the questions posed deal with the process dimension of strategy and are of a real dynamic nature. Porter labels this as the longitudinal problem in strategy research in which the process by which firms attain a superior position is investigated. Below I will briefly sketch for each of the successive links in figure 10.1 the key determinants of firm success as proposed by Porter and the framework used.

Figure 10.1: Towards the origin of competitive advantage of firms, Porter's chain of causality framework.

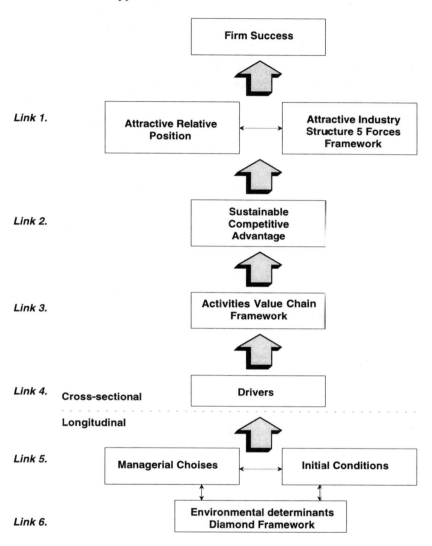

Source: Author, adapted from Porter (1991, figure 2)

Link 1: *firm success is a function of industry structure and of its relative position in that industry*

The question "Why are firms successful?" can be answered by observing two determinants at the industry level: (1) the attractiveness of the industry structure as such and (2) the attractiveness of the relative position of a firm vis-à-vis its rivals; see link 1 in figure 10.1. Porter contributed to understanding this link by his very wellknown Five Forces framework discussed in chapters 2 and 3. With that framework it is possible to analyze the industry structure and to determine the competitive forces that explain the sustainability or the degree of sustainability of profits of firms. However, as Porter (1991, p. 101) observes: "An attractive position is, of course, an outcome and not a cause". The question becomes "why, or how did the attractive position arise?" This link gives rise to the second link in figure 10.1.

Link 2:   *Firm success is a function of a sustainable competitive advantage*

This second link deals with the question of the determinants of a sustainable competitive advantage. According to Porter in his book *Competitive Strategy* of 1980, there are two basic types of competitive advantage: lower costs compared to the rivals and the ability to differentiate and earn a premium price that exceeds the additional costs of differentiation. He adds a third determinant, scope, because competitive advantage cannot be examined without considering competitive scope, such as the choice of products and demand segments served and the degree of vertical integration. So link 2 offers three determinants: cost, differentiation and scope. But again, delving deeper, the question arises where do these advantages regarding cost, differentiation and scope come from? How can we understand the cost position of firms? Why are there differences with respect to differentiation strategies between firms within the same industry? This type of questions brings us to link 3 in figure 10.1.

Link 3:   *Firm success grows out of discrete activities*

This third link proposes as determinants of firm success the value chain and value system and particular discrete activities and linkages between activities. These concepts are developed in Porter's book of 1985 *Competitive Advantage: creating and sustaining superior performance* and briefly discussed here among others in chapter 4. Looking from this "activity perspective" a firm's strategy defines its configuration of activities and how these activities are interconnected by linkages. From this perspective the determinants of the preceding link can be explained. As Porter (1991, p. 102) observes: "Competitive advantage results from a firm's ability to perform the required activities at a collectively lower cost than rivals or perform some activities in unique ways that create buyer value and hence allow the firm to command a ways that create buyer value and hence allow the firm to command a premium price. The required mix and configuration of activities, in turn, is altered by competitive scope." An attractive aspect of this "activity perspective", in my opinion, is the challenge to analyze strategically relevant activities outside the boundary of the firm involved as well. For example, buyers of the firm products have value chains as well. Investigating how these buyers perform their activities related to the firm's product or service increases the understanding of potential sources of differentiation for the firm's own product or service. If firm success grows out of discrete activities, again the question can be raised what are the determinants of the discrete activities and linkages of a value chain? Why are some firms able to perform particular activities in such a way that it creates more value than the rivals? This leads to the next link.

Link 4:   Firm success grows out of drivers
The fourth link in the chain of causality proposes drivers as determinants of firm success. According to Porter (1991, p. 104): "Drivers are structural determinants of differences among competitors in the cost of the buyer of activities or group of activities." The same set of drivers determines both the relative cost of activities and differentiation possibilities. Examples of the most important drivers of competitive advantage in a particular activity are the scale at which the activity is performed, cumulative learning in the activity, the ability to share the activity with other units within the firm. This last example plays a role in the preceding chapter 4 on corporate strategy. Porter stresses the fact that delving to the level of the drivers, increases our understanding of the sustainability of competitive advantage: drivers constitute the underlying forces of competitive advantage. But again, the question can be raised what are the determinants of these drivers? Why do firms achieve superior positions vis-à-vis the drivers in the value chain? To answer these questions we must "cross the barrier", that is the dotted line in figure 10.1. We cannot any longer operate within the static approach of analyzing firm success given a competitive position. We must focus now on the process by which superior positions are attained. This leads us to the fifth link.

Link 5:   Firm success grows out of initial conditions and managerial choices
Porter proposes two determinants of this fifth link: firm's initial conditions and managerial choices. These initial conditions may reside

within the firm, such as skills, and outside the firm in its business environment. Managerial choices define, according to Porter, the firm's concept for competing, its configuration of activities and the supporting investments in assets and skills. These two determinants can be interrelated. As Porter (1991, p. 106) observes: "Earlier choices, which have led to the current pool of internal skills and assets, are a reflection of the external environment surrounding the firm at the time. The earlier one pushes back in the chain of causality, the more it seems that successive managerial choices and initial conditions external to the firm govern outcomes." These initial conditions external to the firm give rise to the next and last link in figure 10.1.

Link 6:   *Firm success grows out of the four determinants of the diamond framework*

Although Porter (1991) in his graphical representation of the chain of causality framework ends with link five, he points out: "The environment, via the diamond, affects both a firm's initial conditions and its managerial choices." and "The diamond, then, begins to address a dynamic theory of strategy early in the chain of causality." (p. 114-115). That is why I add a sixth link in figure 10.1 showing the business environment as depicted by the diamond framework discussed in chapter 6. However, this last link in the search for the origins of a firm's competitive advantage raises again a very fundamental question: "Does the competitive advantage reside in the business environment or in the firm?"

Does the business environment as the origin of competitive advantage eliminate the role of strategy?
On the basis of Porter (1991) a brief answer to this provoking question can be given: No! As Porter (1991, p. 110) stresses: "Competitive advantage, then, may reside as much in the environment as in the individual firm." Although the environment is shaped over time through a process of mutual reinforcement of the four diamond determinants, firms play a key role in this process as well. As Porter stresses in his book *The competitive advantage of nations*, firms must work actively to improve their home base by upgrading the determinants. Indeed, a firm has a strategic stake in making its home base or diamond a better platform for international competitive success. But in doing so "causality becomes blurred". The determinants of the diamond framework influence managerial conditions and are deliberately influenced by firms. That is why in figure 10.1 I connect

link 5 and 6 in an interacting way. Hence, the origins of competitive advantage reside over time both in the business environment and in the firm itself. Managers must understand and benefit from their business environment by deliberately upgrading the environmental determinants of competitive advantage. As this challenge is not perceived by all firms in a certain industry within a particular region or nation, differences in international competitive success of these firms come into being, as has been shown in Porter's *Competitive advantage of nations* book.

Having concluded that the origins of competitive advantage reside over time both in the environment and in the firm, Porter raises a few unanswered questions; the first two of his questions I will mention. The first question deals with the *balance* between environmental determinism and strategic choice in creating a firm's competitive advantage. According to Porter, it is still unclear in how far a company is able to pick its own strategy and in how far the environment determines a company's success. His second unanswered question deals with the widely observed phenomenon of the degree of stickiness or *inertia* in competitive positions once a firm stops progressing. How important is a firm's existing competitive position vis-à-vis its ability to renew? Although both questions are very intriguing, empirical research based on Porter (1991) is scarce. This stimulated me and my co-author Warmerdam to apply a part of Porter's chain of causality framework to a successful international Dutch firm, thus illustrating the origins of the competitive advantage of this firm and the inertia in its competitive positions. Based on our research (Van den Bosch & Warmerdam, 1994, 1995) it appears that Porter's chain of causality framework can contribute to finding interesting answers to the questions raised above. For example, in our empirical research we found that the balance between environmental determinism and strategic choice (Porter's first question) can change over time.

Conclusion

The question "Why are firms successful?" is one of the basic questions in strategy. However, the strategy literature contains a lot of different frameworks with different time perspectives at different levels of analysis, each providing different answers pertaining to the origin of competitive advantage. This lack of theoretical coherence is recognized as one of the basic problems in strategy research. Furthermore, the necessity to improve our understanding of the nature of strategic change and of the process dimension of strategy in particular stresses the importance to take time seriously in strategy research. In fact, dynamic theories of strategies are still in their infancy (Van den Bosch, 1995). Therefore, a real challenge for strategy research is the development of more general and in particular dynamic strategy frameworks aimed at explaining the question "Why are firms successful *over* time?".

After having developed different, widely appreciated strategy frameworks on various levels of analysis, Porter delivered another contribution to strategy theory with his chain of causality framework. In my opinion, this contribution shows that indeed it is possible to develop integrated and dynamic strategy frameworks that make sense from a dual perspective. Indeed, both practitioners and strategy researchers can benefit from Porter's chain of causality framework. Practitioners can try to understand, benefit and influence the determinants of their firm's success over time. Strategy researchers can keep searching for the origins of competitive advantage of firms, thereby taking Porter's chain of causality framework as a very interesting and important point of departure.

References

Bosch, F.A.J. van den, 1995. *What makes time strategic?*, Management Report Series, no. 219, Rotterdam School of Management, Rotterdam.

Bosch, F.A.J. van den, P.C.T. Warmerdam, 1994. Towards a dynamic theory of strategy: the importance of a longitudinal analysis of the sustainability of the competitive advantage of firms, Paper presented at the 14th Annual Strategic Management Society Conference, Jouy-en-Josas, France.

_____, 1995. Naar een dynamische theorie van strategie, de bijdrage van Porter's-diamant model (Towards a dynamic theory of strategy: the contribution of Porter's diamond framework), *Bedrijfskunde*, vol. 67, no. 1, p. 62-69.

Porter, M.E., 1991, Towards a Dynamic Theory of Strategy, *Strategic Management Journal*, vol. 12, p. 95-117.

List of contributors

Prof.Dr. F.A.J. van den Bosch is professor of Management, chairman of the Department of Strategic Management and Business Environment, Rotterdam School of Management, Erasmus University Rotterdam.

Dr. T. Elfring is associate professor of Business Environment and Strategy at the same department.

Mr. L.A. Geelhoed is Secretary General of the Dutch Ministry of Economic Affairs, the Hague, The Netherlands.

Drs. C.A.J. Herkströter is, since 1992, chairman of Committee of managing Directors of the Royal Dutch/Shell group, the Hague, The Netherlands.

Prof. Drs. F.A. Maljers was co-chairman of Unilever N.V. from 1984 to 1994; he is currently professor of Strategic Management of Multinational Companies of the Department of Strategic Management and Business Environment and, among others, chairman of the supervisory board of Philips Electronics N.V.

Dr. A.P. de Man worked at the Department of Strategic Management and Business Environment as Research Associate until 1996 and is currently a consultant at KPMG Management Consultancy, Amstelveen, The Netherlands.

Drs. R.J.H. Meijer is assistant professor of Strategic Management at the Department of Strategic Management and Business Environment, Rotterdam School of Management.

Drs. R.M. Smit was alderman of the city of Rotterdam responsible for the port until 1996 and currently is Director General of the Dutch Ministry of Internal Affairs, the Hague, The Netherlands.

Dr. H. Volberda is associate professor of Strategic Management at the Department of Strategic Management and Business Environment, Rotterdam School of Management.

Dr. B de Wit was assistant professor of Strategic Management at the Department of Strategic Management and Business Environment and is currently professor at the Maastricht School of Management.

Subject Index